# How to be Psychic

# How to be Psychic

*Sasha Fenton*

ZAMBEZI PUBLISHING LTD

Published:
in the UK, copyright © 2003 by Zambezi Publishing Ltd
P.O. Box 221 Plymouth,
Devon PL2 2YJ (UK)
www.zampub.com     email: info@zampub.com
and in the USA in 2003 by Sterling Publishing Co., Inc.,

British Library Cataloguing in Publication Data:
A catalogue record for this book
is available from the British Library

ISBN 978-1-903065-25-9

Illustrations & typesetting by Jan Budkowski
Reprinted 2009
by Lightning Source UK
35798642

*Disclaimer*

This book is intended to provide information regarding the subject matter, and to
entertain. The contents are not exhaustive and no warranty is given as to accuracy
of content. The book is sold on the understanding that neither the publisher not the
author are thereby engaged in rendering professional services, in respect of the
subject matter or any other field. If expert guidance is required, the services of a
competent professional should be sought.

The reader is urged to read a range of other material on the book's subject
matter, and to tailor the information to his individual needs. Neither the author nor
the publisher shall have any responsibility to any person or entity regarding any loss
or damage caused or alleged to be caused, directly or indirectly, by the use or misuse
of information contained in this book. If you do not wish to be bound by the above,
you may return this book in sound condition to the publisher, with its receipt, for a
refund of the purchase price.

# About the Author

Sasha Fenton was born in Bushey, near Watford in Hertfordshire, England, and many members of her family have had an interest in psychic or occult subjects. Sasha became interested in palmistry in childhood, partly due to the fact that her mother knew something about it, although Sasha learned her craft initially from books and later by studying people's hands directly.

In her twenties, Sasha read and learned all she could about astrology, and by the time of her Saturn return (around the age of 30), Sasha was writing up horoscopes for clients. She soon added Tarot reading to her list of skills.

Sasha is a past Secretary and President of the British Astrological and Psychic Society (BAPS), a past chairman of the British Advisory Panel on Astrological Education and a past member of the Executive Council of the Writers' Guild of Great Britain.

Together with her husband Jan Budkowski, Sasha started Zambezi Publishing in 1998 and they now produce books written by a variety of skilled practitioners in the mind, body and spirit fields.

**For more information, visit Sasha's website at :**
**www.sashafenton.com**

# Contents

# 1

## What will you find in this Book?

In this book I will show you various methods and techniques for psychic development that you can try for yourself.

The first part of my book contains basic information and some techniques that will keep you safe while doing psychic work. Then, we go on to look at a variety of psychic methods. I explain each of these and give you exercises that you can do yourself. Some of these experiments require more than one person, so you can look forward to having some fun with your friends while trying them out.

I have enlivened many of the topics with stories that my psychic friends have passed on to me - occasionally changing the names and details where the subject matter is sensitive.

There is nothing dangerous in this book, but opening yourself up to psychic awareness can lead to strange dreams or uncomfortable feelings, so I make a point at the outset of showing you how to close down after doing anything of a psychic nature. In some cases, developing psychic awareness can save you from problems in your everyday life, because you will pick up early warning signals about people or situations that might be harmful. I even show you how to turn back spite and malice to the person who sends it to you - without harming either yourself or them.

There are many reasons why someone is drawn to investigate psychic and spiritual matters. Some discover a deep need for spirituality, others find that they are drawn to make use of a talent that they suddenly discover. Many are just fascinated. The main cause of fear and hatred in connection with any form of psychism is ignorance, so by showing you what is involved, your own nervousness about these subjects will soon fade.

Writing about these nebulous subjects in a clear and logical manner is not easy, and the area that the world of spirit, ESP and the paranormal covers is huge. In this book, I have tackled as many subjects as I can think of, and included many exercises that should work - if not at once, perhaps after the second or third try. I suggest that you read the whole book and then turn back to those topics that interest you most.

Not everybody can develop in the same way. Some become clairvoyants and message receivers, others can see auras or even move objects around with their minds. Some are natural trance mediums, while others are healers. Not everyone wants to do everything, and some have a narrow band of interest - but others want to know about it all.

Whatever direction you end up taking, this book will stand as a starting point for all who are interested in taking the road to discovery.

# 2

## Do you have the Potential?

People don't waste time reading books on subjects that hold no interest for them, so if you are reading this, the chances are that you have something going for you. Nobody makes a financial commitment to buy a book that they don't want, so if you have bought this (rather than picking it up at a friend's house), then you are clearly being drawn towards investigating these subjects. In addition, there is a saying in psychic circles that, if a person wants to learn, a teacher and a source of information will present itself. It is clear that something guides the person to take steps on the road to knowledge, so let us grasp the most difficult nettle in the patch and ask who or what may be guiding you.

There are various possible answers. For example, some outside force may be responsible. Different people view this force as a spiritual guide, a guardian angel or some kind of partial or wholly religious or godly force. Some say that the universe is directing them, while others consider that their long dead ancestors are pushing them to develop their talents. Some say that their own higher-consciousness or intuition is prodding them. At this stage, I suggest that you don't worry too much about where the urge is coming from, but just go with the flow and see what happens.

### *Are some people more likely to be psychic than others?*
I have known psychics who have had an idyllic childhood, but these people usually grew up in households where psychic ability

was taken for granted. In other circumstances, an idyllic childhood is not the best background for psychism, because those things that make a growing child unhappy, lonely or resentful, tend to aid the development of intuition.

A child who grows up in some wild place soon learns to keep half an eye open for dangerous animals, snakes, biting insects and so on. A child who lives in a large city soon learns how to cross a road without being run over - and to avoid places where madmen lurk. It is a sad fact that most of the children who are abducted by killers come from good families where they have never learned to fear adults. A child who grows up in difficult circumstances, or who finds it hard to win the approval of parents and other adults, or who is treated as an outsider by other children, soon learns to keep a weather eye out for trouble. These lessons may start out as conscious things, but eventually they become second nature and they sow the seeds of intuition. The child who is the apple of everyone's eye may have some measure of intuition, but without abrasion, this is unlikely to develop very far.

Even when a childhood is reasonable, a deeply unhappy marriage or a prolonged period of stress and worry can help a person's intuition to develop. Every bad situation has one or two silver linings, as they can be character building. Ask anyone who has survived a difficult or traumatic situation, and they will tell you that this was when they developed knowledge, skills, strengths and abilities of which they were previously unaware. They may not know it, but this is also when their intuition took a great leap forward. The following tale is both true and typical.

### *Jackie's third eye opens*

Jackie and her mother were very close. It wasn't surprising really, because Jackie was an only child and her father had left the family when she was small. Jackie's mum liked to make the occasional visit to a clairvoyant. This was partly to reassure herself that she was making the right decisions in her life, and partly to see if there might be something nice somewhere over the horizon. Jackie's mother went out to work, so although Jackie's childhood was not unpleasant, it was a somewhat lonely one. Jackie loved to read, and time spent sitting around quietly helped her to develop her imagination.

Puberty brought a sudden awakening, because when Jackie was fourteen, she had a frightening out-of-body experience, and this was soon followed by a number of other inexplicable experiences. Much later, Jackie went through a period of intense struggle, brought on by an acrimonious divorce, a lack of support for herself and her children, the loss of her home and severe financial hardship. Jackie worked during the day, but during her lonely evenings, she began to read books on psychic matters, and to study the Tarot. Soon, other people began to persuade Jackie to give them Tarot readings, and this progressed until she was working on a semi-professional basis. She then obtained a diploma in candle magic through a correspondence course, and whenever she could spare the money, she attended spiritualist and psychic events and seminars.

It was while she was at one of these that she met a well-known man who was a medium and a healer. A supportive friendship grew between this elderly man and Jackie, and he gradually taught her all that she needed in order to set her feet on the path of work as a psychic medium and healer. Soon, Jackie qualified as a Reiki healer and a Tarot Consultant. Jackie now performs channeling sessions at Spiritualist churches, and she lectures on psychic subjects. She has turned her love of writing to good use, and started yet another part-time profession as an author.

### So how can you develop your potential?

There is no magic potion or exercise that will endow instant psychic talent. As with any skill, it takes time and effort for these to develop. Some people suggest that doing yoga will help, but while it is possible that such mental and physical exercises can be an aid to awareness, I suggest that if you like doing yoga, do it for its own sake rather than as an aid to psychism.

Not every sensitive person has the same kind of psychic gift. The most common effect is to feel things or to be aware of things on a subliminal level, but some people are definite psychic receptors, while others are physical mediums who can move things around with their minds. Some see auras; others see ghosts, while many are healers or mediums who can bridge the gap between the living and those who have passed over.

### Checklist

Just for the fun of it, here is a checklist that you can use in order to examine your own encounters and beliefs.

I haven't included every possibility that exists, but I have tried to pick out those that are fairly common. There is no particular score that proves that you are psychic, because any one of these things will demonstrate some measure of ESP.

Consider each question, and tick each box that applies to you.

| Your Experience | Tick |
|---|---|
| You wrote to a friend, and your letter crossed in the mail with one that your pal sent you. | |
| You thought of a friend, and that friend then telephoned you. | |
| You were driving a car when you suddenly felt uneasy, so you slowed down. Then, around the corner, you came across an accident or something else that you couldn't have known about in advance. | |
| You felt that what appeared to be a perfectly reasonable person couldn't be trusted, and you were later proved to be right. | |
| You felt uneasy when in a particular house or place. | |
| You went after a job that looked great on the face of things, but you didn't take it because you had a "funny feeling" about it. | |
| You felt that you should soon start looking for another job, despite the fact that your current one appeared to be all right. | |
| You felt uneasy about an adult who was attached to your child's friend - to the point where you didn't want your child spending time in the other child's house. | |
| You knew something was wrong with a loved one, even though they were at a distance and you had no reason to suspect anything. | |
| You felt some kind of presence when there was nobody around. | |

| Your Experience | Tick |
|---|---|
| You have "seen" a relative or friend who has died - either at the point of their death or some time afterwards. | |
| You have heard knocking or strange sounds when there was no reason for them. | |
| You lost something, but had a strange feeling that it was stolen; you may even have an idea about who had taken it. | |
| You have felt that you knew a place that you have never visited before, or you feel drawn to a particular place for no logical reason. | |
| You have had a near-death experience. | |
| You meet someone, perhaps of a completely different culture, age group, background, yet you feel a strange, immediate kind of kinship. | |
| You make a new friend, start to explore your past and discover that you have both done similar things. | |
| Some of your dreams come true. | |
| You felt that something was going to happen, and then it did. | |
| You have experienced poltergeist activity or something else that was hard to explain. | |
| You have touched a sick person or just sat and talked with them, and they felt better afterwards. | |
| You have touched a sick animal and it recovered quickly. | |
| You have found that a particular room or part of a room felt unusually cold when there was no reason for it. | |
| You have seen odd things out of the corner of your eye or heard mumbled voices as you fell asleep. | |
| You have had a vision of someone who has passed over. | |

# 3

# Attitude

There are many kinds of impulse that can drive a person to take an interest in psychic matters, and while some of them may appear more admirable than others, in my opinion, most are acceptable. Obviously, the desire to help others or to discover more about the strange world that we live in are acceptable notions, but I don't have any problem with those who wish to be seen as "special", or with those who wish to earn money through sittings.

We all want to be special, and that is fair enough - but if you wish to be seen as a superior kind of being by others, or to unnerve them by your wonderful gifts, the gifts (and your friends) will soon melt away. If you want to earn money by giving clairvoyant readings or by other similar means, treat yourself to my book, "Prophecy for Profit" as this shows you how to make a success of this kind of work.

### Negative vibes

There are some people who use psychic abilities or who threaten to use them in order to frighten, control or influence others. There are some slimy types who use their gifts in order to gain sexual favors or some kind of sexual advantage. Needless to say, this is not the kind of behavior that anybody would advocate. Curses, bad vibes and any other unworthy activity will always bounce back and hurt the perpetrator.

It is worth bearing in mind that there is a spiritual element in psychic work that isn't obvious in any other kind of endeavor. We all know how we should behave, and the Christian idea of "Do unto others as you would be done by," is probably as good advice as any. If there isn't at least some spiritual element in your motivation, psychic work cannot benefit you in the long run - and this applies as much to professional psychics as it does to amateurs. You don't need to belong to any specific religion to be spiritual, but on the other hand, you don't need to give up any religion that you already adhere to. You may believe in reincarnation, or you may not.

If you wish to work in the psychic field, you will need to keep an eye on your moral and ethical behavior in other areas of your life as well. By this, I don't mean spurning a night of passion with a stranger, giving up eating cream cakes or doing without money, but I do mean being honest in your dealings. Be fair to others and treat them as you would like to be treated. Don't take advantage of employees, or welch on business deals, and don't take advantage of those who are vulnerable. Those who work in the psychic arena are more open to karmic retribution than others, so why ask for trouble?

I have heard of psychics who frighten their clients by suggesting that a member of their family is likely to fall sick, and then offering to light candles, say special prayers or perform clearances at an inflated price. Don't even think about doing anything of this kind.

### Winning money

I have always been psychic and I have trained myself to make the most of my natural gifts - but how do I fare with the lottery or on horse races? I have never won anything on the British lottery, and neither do I have any more luck than the next person does on the rare occasions when I put a small bet on a horse or buy a raffle ticket. I have had the occasional small win, but not as a result of anything other than sheer chance.

I have heard of people who do win by using their psychic gifts ending up with all their winnings and more being taken away from them. I once heard of a case where a man used witchcraft in order to gain a specific amount of money. He got his money - but as compensation for losing a leg in a traffic accident! Personally, I prefer to keep both my legs and to work for my money. This was a case of black magic indeed. If you are in real need, ask your spiritual guides to send you what you need. It is also perfectly permissible to perform candle-burning rituals for this purpose. The chances are that you will be given what you need - or better still, that you will be given the opportunity to earn what you need. Once you have received this, always give something back to spirit by giving a little money to someone who needs it.

Here is a wonderful story that my friend, Seldiy Bate told me. She once desperately needed a particular sum of money and she focused her mind on obtaining it. A few days later while she was out shopping, she found some Monopoly money lying in the road. When she picked it up she discovered that it was the exact sum that she needed! A couple of weeks later, she had an opportunity to do some work that brought her the sum she required in real money. This was clearly "spirit" showing its sense of humor.

### *Do you need to become a vegetarian?*

The modern interest in spirituality took off in the early 1970s, when the Beatles visited India and brought the Maharishi Mahesh Yogi back with them. In a very short space of time, Hindu and Buddhist ideas flooded the psychic world, bringing vegetarianism with them, and many folk became vegetarian or even vegan as a result. If you believe that we are able to reincarnate in and out of the animal world, you may naturally not wish to eat flesh of any kind. If you believe that eating meat will block your more subtle glands or your chakras, you may wish to become vegetarian. Most professional psychics seem to be carnivores, so to my mind it is not necessary to become a vegetarian unless you particularly want to. Having said this, it is not easy to perform psychic work after a heavy meal, and meat does seem to lie on the stomach for a while. It may be better

to eat a light veggie meal or a salad, do your work, and to enjoy
your meat meal later.

### *Drink, drugs and alcohol*

It is true that one very small drink can be helpful, as this allows the
normal self-censoring part of the brain to relax, but if you intend
doing much psychic work or to become professional, it is better not to
use alcohol in this way. Having a drink with a meal or in the normal
social sense is fine, but if it becomes a regular part of your efforts to
become psychic, you will become a drunk rather than a psychic.

There was a fashion during the 1970s to use cannabis, LSD and
magic mushrooms as a means of expanding the mind and the inner
universe. No professional psychic takes any such drugs, so they are
clearly unnecessary. Some spiritual people are so into alternative
therapies that they won't even take an over-the-counter tablet for a
headache, but others use normal medical drugs in the normal way,
when necessary.

In the past, practically every adult smoked, but now very few do
so. It is a fact that many mediums were (and some still are) heavy
smokers. One medium told me that many of them find cigarette
smoking a way of protecting their vulnerable auras. Please don't
become a smoker if you aren't one already, because giving it up is
one of the hardest things on earth to do! Smoking will neither help
nor hinder your psychic training, and there are many other ways of
protecting your aura.

### *Mental illness*

Psychic work won't bring on mental illness. Those who are already
paranoid, neurotic or schizophrenic may focus on psychic matters
as the cause of their illness, or they may accuse it of exacerbating
it, but it is not so. Neurotics will always find something to obsess
about, and if they choose to focus on psychism rather than
hypochondria or some other kind of obsession, they will become
just as boring and annoying to others. Those who are mentally sick
or self-obsessed cannot make good psychics, because being

psychic involves being able to take an interest in other people, rather than just in oneself.

### *Paranoia and the gas fire*

When Jan and I bought our present home, there was a hideous gas fire in the living room. On the odd occasion when we did try to use it, we found it difficult to light, and it smelled. I swore that it smelled "gassy" even when it wasn't in use and I often found myself looking suspiciously at it. One day, I called in a gasman to do some other work in the house, and while he was with us, I asked him to check the fire. He found no gas leaks. I insisted that he check it again, and he began to look at me as if I were crazy. I still felt uneasy, so after the gas man left, Jan and I gave in to my feelings and replaced the ugly monstrosity with an attractive electric fire.

Months later, my aunt, Marjie, told me a similar story in which she had also smelled whiffs of gas coming from a fire in her living room. She called in a gasman who checked her fire and the surrounding pipes with his instruments. Nothing showed up. He began to say that she was crazy - in much the same way that my gasman had suggested to me. My aunt was so sure that something was wrong that she forced the issue and insisted that the gasman check the pipes in the old-fashioned way, by smearing them with soapy water. Sure enough, gas bubbles emerged from a minute crack in the pipes.

Whether I really did smell gas or whether "spirit" was warning me of an impending problem is hard to say, but now we have a great looking fire and the headaches that we suffered from all last winter have gone. Paranoid or psychic? Perhaps both, but ignoring my gut feeling might have ended up costing lives.

### *Materialism versus spiritualism*

I mentioned in the previous chapter that many of the ideas that have permeated modern spiritual thinking came from India. One of the ideas that were often rammed down the throats of aspiring psychics was that materialism was bad and that we should not become attached to money and possessions. Many Asians have come from backgrounds of poverty and are therefore pretty materialistic, so perhaps that is the reason why their clergy are so against materialism. My feeling is that either too much materialism or too much spirituality will lead to an imbalance. Common sense and the middle way are best.

Throughout history, there have been people who have given up the material world in order to concentrate on spiritual matters. St. Francis of Assisi is an obvious example, but there have always been hermits, prophets, Sufis, monks, nuns and other religious people who have turned their backs on society. Many ministers of religion live in relative poverty while they serve their community. If you wish to rid yourself of all material things, please feel free to do so, but it is not a prerequisite.

Most of us need to live a normal life and to have a certain amount of comfort and material success to be happy. I believe that giving a little time and effort to those who need it can't do any harm on a spiritual level. Donating to third world governments usually only serves to swell their leaders' funds in the Swiss banking system, but giving a real helping hand to someone who needs it makes everyone's life better.

### Charging for services rendered

Professionals charge; this is a fact of life. If you don't believe me, try consulting a lawyer, accountant, a marriage guidance counselor or any other service-provider. Despite this, there are people around who maintain that a psychic should give his time for nothing. When I was surviving as a "reader" and some know-all commented that I should work for nothing, I used to say that when my gas, electricity, milk, groceries, petrol, motor repairs bills, local taxes, and mortgage came my way for free, I would consider dropping my charges. I have no problem with those who wish to give readings or sittings free of charge, and as it happens, I have never charged anyone for spiritual healing, mainly because I don't do it very often.

On the other hand, if it were my main line of work, then of course I would charge for it.

### A personal checklist

Look into your heart and fill in as many ticks as you like on the checklist. All the answers are fine, apart from the last two. If you feel that you are even marginally drawn to the ideas in the last two, give up psychic work before you hurt others and get hurt in return.

| Your Motives | Tick |
|---|---|
| Psychic subjects fascinate you and you want to know more. | |
| You have had some psychic experiences. | |
| You have always felt different and you want to discover why. | |
| You have always been able to see or feel a little way into the future. | |
| You want to help people by psychic means. | |
| You want to become more spiritual. | |
| You want to be a little special. | |
| You already give readings of some kind and you want to add a psychic element to your work. | |
| You want to earn money by giving readings or sittings. | |
| You feel that you have a healing gift. | |
| You want to get back at those who have hurt you. | |
| You want to make others do what you want, or you wish to control them. | |

### *Status and opinions*

Don't allow your gifts to go to your head, and don't become so carried away with yourself that you believe you are better than others are. I have known mediums who consider themselves better than Tarot readers, and astrologers who consider themselves better than mediums. Some people learn a little about our subject, consider that they have the answer to everything, and start to make pompous or fatuous remarks. Sure, you will soon know a few things, but others know a lot about various other subjects, so live and let live - and always keep a sense of humor.

# 4

## Psychic Training

Most spiritualist churches and psychic centers have development circles attached to them. If you try one group and don't like the vibe, look around for another. Some witchcraft covens offer training. Specialist magazines advertise courses on Tarot, palmistry and astrology. Check everything out before diving into it. If possible contact one or two people who have studied with a particular group or through a correspondence course and see what they have to say about it.

Not everybody wants to train through a spiritualist church, witchcraft group or any other kind of organization and not everyone should do so. It may be better for you to read about these subjects, try things for yourself and develop in your own way. You may start by learning to read the Tarot or using some other method of developing your intuition. Read books by a wide variety of authors and attend events, seminars, talks, psychic and mystic festivals or anything else of the kind. You will make like-minded friends and you will soon discover more avenues. Don't take everything you hear as gospel. Sift all that you read, mull over the ideas, concepts and opinions that others tell you about, and then work out in your own mind what is real and what isn't.

I have never had any formal training of any kind. My mother was mildly interested in palmistry and various members of my family had prophetic dreams or strong feelings that they followed up on. I took an interest in palmistry and then became an astrologer and a Tarot reader. I spent many years giving readings for clients on what I considered to be purely practical lines before I realized that I was psychic. When I began to work among others who used mainly psychic or spiritual techniques, they encouraged me to use these myself. I slowly came to believe in and rely upon my own psychic gifts, so that these are now as important to me as everything else that I do.

### A worthwhile lesson

A teacher of psychic studies called Berenice Watt once said to me that the first thing anybody should teach their students is how to close down after a session, so that they don't walk around in a state of vulnerability. She said that many people who had trained with other psychic teachers came to her for help because they were being "spooked" due to their new openness. I agree totally - but it seems logical that one has to learn how to open up before learning how to close down. When I teach psychic development at workshops, I start by showing my students how to open up and close down before I do anything else.

### Opening the chakras

The word chakra is a Hindu word, pronounced "char-kra" with a hard "char", something like the word, "charcoal". This word means wheel, and it is actually the symbol that sits in the center of the Indian national flag. The Hindus tell us that there are 78,000 chakras that are spread around the body, but we need only to concern ourselves with seven of these for the moment.

Five of the chakras go through the body from front to back at specific points along the spine, while the sixth is in the center of the forehead and the last is on the crown of the head.

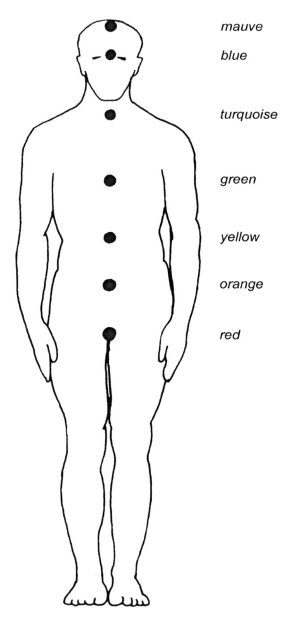

mauve

blue

turquoise

green

yellow

orange

red

*The seven major chakras*

The colors of the chakras are the same as the colors in a rainbow:
- The crown chakra is purple or mauve.
- The forehead chakra (or third eye) is dark blue.
- The throat chakra is light turquoise blue.
- The heart chakra (around the breastbone area) is green.
- The spleen chakra (the area of the diaphragm) is yellow.
- The solar-plexus chakra (the middle of the abdomen) is orange.
- The base chakra (at the base of the spine) is red.

### *Exercise: Opening the chakras*

My friend, Barbara Ellen showed me this method for opening the chakras:

Imagine yourself gathering light from the whole universe, and then bring this light down to the crown chakra.

See the crown chakra as a purple lotus (water lily) and imagine it opening and allowing the light to enter through it.

Then, allow the light to come down as far as the forehead chakra, at which point a large blue eye opens up.

Allow the light to come down as far as the throat, at which point a pale blue flower opens up.

Allow the light to come down to the heart chakra where a bunch of green leaves opens up.

Allow the light to come down to the spleen chakra and let a large yellow daisy or dahlia open up.

Allow the light to come down to the solar-plexus chakra where a large orange marigold opens up.

Allow the light to come down to the base chakra, where a big red poppy opens up.

Finally, allow the light to filter down through the legs and to fill out the whole body and the surrounding aura.

Finish by imagining the light extending down into the bowels of the earth.

### Closing the chakras

All one has to do is to reverse the procedure. Start by imagining the light that has reached down into the earth being turned off. Then turn off the light in your legs until you reach the base chakra. Now turn off the light there and carefully close down the read poppy. Now turn off the light up to and beyond the solar plexus and close that flower down tightly. Continue the process until you have finished, and then send the light off into the universe.

### Quick fixes and other methods

Water is indeed a wonderful way of clearing the system. If you are concerned that you may have attracted something spooky - and especially so if you have been giving spiritual healing - try ending your day by taking a good shower. Don't forget to give your hair and even the soles of your feet a thorough scrub. While you are standing under the shower, imagine clear, pure spiritual water entering your body through the crown of your head and flooding through you and out again through your fingers and toes. Later, when you go to bed, imagine yourself climbing into a sleeping bag with a reflective silver-colored outer surface. Then imagine yourself zipping it up all around you like a cocoon. This will help to protect your aura and enable you to get a good night's sleep.

### What next?

Move on through this book and check it all out, then you may find that one particular aspect of psychic or spiritual work appeals to you more than another. Once you know what interests you, check out magazines, books and the Internet for more information and in order to reach those who work in the field. Don't expect a professional to drop everything and teach you there and then, but some may be happy to suggest where you should look for advice and information. Others are so busy that they won't want to be bothered. If there are talk sites on the Internet where you can ask questions, try using them.

When I was a consultant rather than a publisher, I would occasionally receive phone calls from people who wanted a little information. I was happy to help such people, but some advantage-takers expected me to spend an hour or two on the phone, teaching them all there is to know about their pet subject. There is no way that anyone can learn "all about" these things by phone in a couple of hours and it is selfish to expect someone to give up their time in this way. If you have too much time on your hands, try giving some of it to someone who needs it.

### *Do-it-yourself jobs*

A good option is to gather a few friends around and start your own development circle. Read as many books as you can so that you can drum up ideas for your meetings. Some of the following ideas are courtesy of my friend Jackie, while others are mine.

Open the proceedings with a prayer. You can write your own prayer or you can find something suitable. It should include something that asks for your group to be protected from unpleasant spiritual influences. The prayer should ask that the members should be able to open up and do the work that is needed, and ultimately for their work to benefit others.

You must all open your chakras, then you can designate someone to lead the group on that particular evening and ask them to take the members through a guided meditation. After this, you can select a second person can lead the group through another meditation if you wish. There are plenty of books on meditating, so once you have used up the few ideas that I have suggested in this book, you will find plenty more out there.

After this, the group can sit in pairs, with one acting as "reader" and the other as "client". It may help if each pair holds hands. Now the reader should try to pick up something from the client. Anything may come through, from simply feeling the client's current emotional state to linking with events in their lives or even getting in touch with their family members or friends who have passed over. Change partners after a while and try this again with different pairs. Jackie also suggests that when you swap seats that you try to pick up something from the aura of the person who was previously occupying the seat! When you reach the chapter in this book on psychometry, you will discover lots more ideas that lend themselves to group training experiences.

Jackie suggests that the members should bring a CD of music along and pick out a track that they think might suit one of the other group members. Then the group listens to some of the music and the person who it was for tells the group whether it has any special meaning for them.

The group can try candle scrying or various other forms of creating links as a change from time to time. Another idea is to try automatic writing. You could ask the group to draw something that shows how they feel and then for other members of the group to analyze this. The illustration will generate feelings, as well as suggesting an emotion or a situation by what it represents. Indeed, there are many ideas in this book, from dowsing to ghost busting that the group might like to try for themselves. The group should end the session by closing their chakras and sending the good vibes that remain from their enjoyable evening out via the universe to give healing to all those who need it.

# 5

## To Meditate or Not to Meditate

There are many books that tell us that meditating is good for us, while those who like meditation sometimes exhort us to do so on a daily basis. This ignores the fact that many people find meditation difficult - and dare I say it, boring and not consistently productive.

To my mind, this kind of self-discipline comes into the same category as regular attendance at a gym or going on a strict diet. We know that these things are good for us, but most of us cannot keep it up for very long. If you like meditating and if you want to do it on a regular basis, I am the last person to suggest that you should give up, but if it is not your thing, then don't force yourself to do any more than you need to.

Having said this, some meditations are definitely worth doing, because they specifically link to what you are trying to achieve. For example, until you become so accustomed to psychic work that your chakras spring open at the slightest nudge, it is always worth doing the chakra opening meditation that I described earlier. Even if you don't always remember to open up, you must always remember to close down after any psychic work. You may wish to perform other meditations from time to time, either for a specific purpose or simply in order to relax. Some people consider meditation to be a private matter, but others prefer to meditate in a group with someone leading the meditation for them.

You can meditate at home while sitting comfortably in a chair or while lying in the bath, but you can also do this outside in the open air. You may fancy creating an area in your garden especially for the purpose. The only danger is that you will become so relaxed that you fall asleep, so you must bear this in mind if you decide to meditate in the bath or somewhere really silly like a public park. As always, be sensible and safe. Here are some meditations that you will find useful for your psychic and spiritual development.

### Exercises in meditation
The first exercise is what my friend, Eve Bingham, calls an "intunement". I am sure that Eve made the word up herself, but it is a good one - so let us use it. Eve taught me the following intunement that I always use at the start of any kind of workshop that I run, even when I teach "scientific" subjects like Chinese astrology or palmistry. This intunement is great for those times when you want to take yourself out of the rush and hurry of mundane life and put yourself into the right frame of mind for psychic work.

### Eve Bingham's intunement
• Imagine yourself in a pleasant, sunny wood on a hot day.
• Notice a pathway ahead of you.
• Slowly wander down the path, noticing the flowers and trees along the way.
• Now see a small lake ahead of you, and see the sun shining on its surface.
• Approach the lake and admire its clear, cool water.
• Step into the lake and allow the water to surround you while you float around happily in it for a while.
• Now look around you and see the tools that will help you. These tools may be something practical like books, a crystal ball, Tarot cards or imaginary bags that are filled with knowledge and spiritual energy.
• Gather these tools into your arms and float towards the edge of the lake.

- Step out of the lake and head back up the path, taking your tools with you.
- Enjoy the peace of the woods once again, and then leave it and come back to reality once again, taking the tools that you found in the lake along with you.

### *A river cruise for relaxation*

After doing this meditation, you can allow your mind to wander and see if anything useful emerges. Relax, close your eyes and then imagine yourself on a riverbank. You see a small boat and you climb into it. The boat floats gently down the river. Use your imagination to watch the countryside pass by as you float along. Float around bends and then into an estuary where you can see the open sea ahead of you. If you want to allow your mind to float freely, you can stay in the boat for a while, then when you are ready to return, just pull the boat to the bank and climb out of it. Leave the boat where it is and come back to the real world again.

### *Preparing to meditate*

Many meditations are easier to perform if you use the same principles that apply to hypnotism before you tackle the meditation itself.

- Imagine yourself at the top of a moving staircase (an escalator to British readers). This staircase is traveling slowly downward. There are no people around and the place is both quiet and safe.
- Step onto the staircase and travel downward while counting down from ten to one.
- Step off the staircase and walk along a short hallway.
- See a second staircase ahead of you and step on to it.
- Travel down this staircase while counting down from ten to one.
- Now step off into a short hallway and notice three doors at the end of the hallway.

• Choose one of the doors to walk through.
• Imagine yourself in a peaceful room.

Bring yourself back by reversing the procedure that I described earlier and by counting up from ten to one on each staircase. Take your time coming back, and don't leap from the chair and start rushing around after you have finished, because you may feel a little "spacey" and disorientated for a while.

While in your relaxed state, you can choose to enter a room and then find all you need to make you psychic. This might include the tools you wish to use or simply to imagine yourself tuning in to your spiritual guides. You can ask to see your spiritual guides and you may start to receive impressions of them. If you have anything on your mind, ask for guidance now. If you want to become more confident, attractive, successful or happier, ask for this now. The chances are that even if you don't get an answer to your questions right away, you may find them later in a dream or in some other way. You will certainly feel more positive, successful and attractive when you ask for help during this kind of meditation.

### *Preparing to meditate by a yoga method*

A second method that I find useful when in the dentist chair or when I can't fall asleep is to send each part of my body to sleep in turn. I call this a yoga meditation because I learned it when I did a lot of yoga when I was a child. If you have a sick child or if anybody you know is sick, unhappy or tense, you can lead them through this meditation, as it will help them to relax and to sleep well.

• Lie down quietly and make yourself comfortable.
• Concentrate on your feet. Clench the muscles in your feet, then relax them and tell them to go to sleep.
• Concentrate on your calves, clench the muscles, release them and tell them to go to sleep.
• Now do the same in turn for your knees, thighs, bottom, hips and back.

- Move to your fingers and do the same, then your hands, lower arms and upper arms.
- Shrug your shoulders hard and relax them, then do this a second and a third time before telling them to relax. This is because the shoulders are often very tense.
- Relax your neck and allow your head to flop where it will before telling it to relax.
- Lastly do the same with your face by screwing it up and releasing it and then telling every part of your face to relax.

Once again, ask to see your guide, spiritual friend, totem animal or anything else that you want to get in touch with at this point. Talk with them if you wish and see if you get any answers or guidance. Even if you get nothing, the chances are that something will come along later in a dream or in some other way, so keep this in mind over the following days.

### *It's all there, in black and white*

My friend, Barbara Ellen, told me this one. It is another meditation that can be used simply for its own sake as a relaxation technique or to open you to psychic impressions. You can relax into it and then just see what comes, or after you have done it, you can ask for guidance, information, and an improvement in your psychic abilities or for anything else that you need.

- Imagine yourself looking at a large blackboard.
- Notice a small white spot in the center of the board.
- The white spot grows slowly until it covers the whole board.
- Now notice a small black spot in the middle of the board.
- The black spot grows slowly until it covers the whole board.
- Do this again with the white spot.
- Now imagine either a black and white yang/yin symbol appearing or a beautiful pink rose in the middle of the board.
- Hold the final image for a while and then relax.

### Pack up your troubles

This meditation was demonstrated to me during a series of classes on the Qabalah, which were given by my friend, Kate Rheeders, in Johannesburg, South Africa. It is a good way of sorting through your problems one at a time and hopefully minimizing them or getting rid of them altogether.

- Once you are relaxed, imagine yourself gathering together several pink plastic garbage bags.
- Consider your greatest problem, pick it up and put it into one of the bags, tie it up and stack it to one side.
- Do the same with your next most pressing problem and so on until you have them all stashed away.
- Then you can choose to imagine yourself floating away on a boat until you reach a spot where you can dump the bags. Row yourself home and leave the problems to float away. Just for once, don't worry about polluting the sea!
- If you don't like water, consider a gentle journey into space and dump the stuff somewhere behind Saturn. This won't harm him - he is used to dealing with problems!

### Cutting ties

There may be someone who you need to stop thinking about or perhaps to get out of your life. This meditation will help you to clear yourself of an attachment that has had its day and that is best put out of your mind.

- Imagine yourself in a large room.
- Take a long length of imaginary ribbon and arrange it in a figure of eight on the floor.
- Imagine yourself sitting within one part of the figure and the other person sitting in the other part.
- Take an imaginary pair of scissors and cut the ribbon where it crosses.

• Imagine the other half of the figure of eight, complete with
the person sitting in it, floating away from you and
disappearing.

### Removing a weighty problem

In a way, this is reminiscent of those religious practices that were
called casting out devils. In this case, it is not bad behavior that you
are trying to cast out but problems and worries that weigh on
someone's mind. This kind of meditation works best when one
person leads another.

If you intend to do this for someone else, start by talking to the
person to discover exactly what is bothering him. Once they start to
open up to you, don't but in - just nod, smile and confirm that you
are really hearing what they are saying to you. When your friend
has finished telling you what ails him, ask him to sit or lay
comfortably somewhere. Use one of the relaxation techniques
outlined above. Once the person is relaxed, put one hand on his
chest, stomach or hold their arm if you don't know them that well,
and then ask your guides and also the other person's guides to come
to your aid. Take the main problem that is on his mind and mentally
ask for it to be physically removed from his body and sent out to
the far side of the universe. Then tackle any lesser problems in the
same way, one at a time.

It may be that neither you nor your friend will be aware of
anything other than relaxation and peace, but it may also be that
you or your friend will see "something" leave his body and fly off.
This may be a kind of gray cobwebby blob, the figure of a person,
a lump of stone or just about anything else. Whatever the thing
might be, it is obviously better out than in.

A friend called Molly did this for me some years ago when my
life was a real mess. While I was lying down in my meditative
condition, I became aware of a heavy weight and then of a lozenge-
shaped, bronze shield almost completely covering me. As Molly
worked on me I felt this heavy thing slowly lift from my body,

hover for a while and they fly through the glass window and vanish into the sky. Afterwards, I felt lighter, happier and more able to cope with all the practical problems that were bothering me. We all have practical problems to deal with in our lives, but we don't need psychic ones as well.

By now you may be wondering how the shield got attached to me. I don't have any real answer, but my feeling is that no person or entity put it there, it was just something that had accumulated over a period of time. The shield probably came from my own psyche, as it seemed to be full of my own fears and self-imposed restrictions. Once it was removed, I could at least take hold of my life and make the changes that I needed. To be sure, life was not all hearts and flowers even after this, but at least I was able to make progress and my circumstances gradually improved. If I ever feel held back or held down by my own inadequacy again, I asked for help, strength and for any new shields that are building up to be removed and sent on their way.

On another occasion, I watched Molly do this for someone else, and this time I saw a black gnome-like creature leave the person and fly off through the window. This kind of healing meditation can really help - so try it for yourself and for others when things are getting on top of you.

### A candle meditation

As luck would have it, I happened to be reading a novel by the British writer, Erin Pizzey, while writing this part of my book. The novel is not on the subject of psychic matters, but it contained this meditation, and it is clear that whoever taught it to Ms Pizzey knew what he was doing. Naturally, the results of the meditation were more dramatic in the novel than they might be in real life, but you never know...

*Light a candle and sit down a few feet away from it. Stare into the flame and allow the light from the candle to become drawn into your body. Allow love, awareness, and spiritual illumination to be drawn into your body along with the candle's light.*

# 6

## Visualization

Visualization spans the gap that exists between meditation and the areas of clairvoyance and spiritual guidance. If you can train your mind's eye to visualize, you will awaken the sector of your brain that is capable of receiving psychic or spiritual messages.

### Exercises: Walking into the picture

Apparently Carl Gustav Jung used to perform the following visualization using a Tarot card. You can select a Tarot card or alternatively, you could use a picture on a calendar, a photograph, and the cover of a book or anything else that has a nice design for this purpose. Carl Jung preferred illustrations of mountains and pathways, but you can use anything that appeals to you.

Sit quietly with your chosen picture in front of you and allow yourself to slip into a slightly dreamy state of mind, then imagine yourself walking into the picture and just see where this takes you. When you finally walk back out again, see if anything has come to you while you were inside the picture. For example, you may have chosen a scene from the American West, which may have brought you a vision that is connected to Native Americans. If you chose a Chinese image, you may receive a message from a Chinese spirit - or you may discover something altogether different. A related idea is to draw a picture of a doorway, look at this and imagine yourself walking through the door, then wait and see what your subconscious mind throws up.

### An amazing exercise

I first read about this exercise in a book by a friend of mine called Zak Martin, but I have tried it many times since and it has usually brought quite astonishing results. This exercise requires two or more people to make it work. Try this out on a small group of friends who are into psychic matters, then you can all do it in turn so that everyone has a chance to see what they can see.

- You need a table, a cloth and several objects of different colors and sizes. You can use anything that comes to hand, such as a selection of ornaments, books, kitchen items, mugs and cups or anything else that is easy to pick up.
- Put the objects on the table and use a cloth or some other means to obscure them.
- Sit your friend or friends at a distance of a couple of yards from the table.
- Ask your friends to quickly open their chakras. Lead them through this if necessary.
- Pick up one object and ask them to stare at it for a few minutes.
- Ask them to close their eyes and hold the vision of the object in their mind's eye. This will not be difficult, because, to some extent, the object will have imprinted itself on their retinas.
- Ask them to tell you when they start to find it more difficult to hold the object in their mind's eye.
- Once they report that the object has all but faded, tell them to open their eyes and look at the object again.
- Repeat this exercise once more by asking them to close their eyes, hold the image and tell you when it starts to fade.
- Ask them to open their eyes for a while and then to close them a third time.

Now, as silently as possible, put the object down and pick up another object from your selection. Ensure that this is a different color and shape to the first.

• Ask your friends to tell you when the object fades. This time they will report the fading effect much more quickly than they did on the previous occasion, and they will find it extremely difficult to hold the image.
• Tell them to keep their eyes closed but to see if they can dredge up a vision of a different color and shape from the one they were seeing previously.

You will be surprised to find that some of them will pick up the new image with the "third eye" alone.

I have seen people describe illustrations of boats with sails, lions or other images that were on the second object. The astonishment of those who discover that they can "see" while their eyes are closed is always something to behold. In my opinion, this is the quickest and most amazing form of awakening for anybody who wants to discover if he or she can pick up something with the "third eye".

### When the material world captures spiritual ideas

It isn't only the psychic and spiritual world that uses visualization techniques, because they pop up in psychology and even in the business world. Management and sales training often includes visualization techniques, such as "seeing yourself making that sale", or seeing your business as a success. Visualizing where we would like ourselves to be in one, two, three or five years hence is a good way of focusing the mind on such material things.

Another good idea is to draw a picture of how you feel at the moment, and then a second that shows how you want to be at some point in the future. None of this will help your psychic studies, but it will help you to focus your mind on what you want to create or what you want your life to become. Drawing an image of your current situation can be a real eye-opener, as it will show you how you feel right now. If you feel bullied, oppressed or in some other way ground down, this will show up graphically in your illustration.

# 7

# Dowsing and Divining

You may be surprised that I suggest that you look into dowsing and divining in a book of this nature, but there are good reasons for this. Dowsing comes easily to many people and we all know that success breeds encouragement. Secondly, unlike other psychic techniques, this is something that you can see happening before your very eyes. It is natural for a student to distrust his first psychic experiences; conversely, when he can see something tangible occurring, it is hard to put it down to an over-active imagination.

Some people find using a pendulum easy, but others do not. I will tell you how to use one later in this chapter, but I don't want you to become frustrated, so I suggest that you start by trying the system with dowsing rods, because many people find them easy to use. I will tell you about a few people whom I have come across who couldn't dowse, a little later in this chapter.

### *Dowsing rods*
Tradition says that water diviners use a forked ash twig, but these are hard to find and I have never even tried to use one. You can buy sets of metal dowsing rods in New Age shops and on the Internet, but some are better than others. Many are fattish copper rods that are bent into a 90-degree angle. Each rod has one long arm and one short one, and the idea is that the dowser holds the short ends and points the long ones forwards. These rods may look nice, but what is really needed is something that will swing around smoothly and

easily. I once came across some wonderful commercially produced rods and then never found any more of their kind. However, I have made many sets of really effective yet simple rods for my students and you can do the same. Homemade rods cost next to nothing, and it is likely that you can find all the parts that you need lying about somewhere in your house.

### *Making a set of dowsing rods*

The following instructions should be carried out with care, and you must bear in mind that everything that you do will be at your own risk. Let common sense and a responsible attitude be your guide. If you have children or others around who are likely to misbehave, then don't do any of the following at all.

#### *The tools that you will require:*
- Two basic wire coat hangers.
- One pair of pliers or some kind of metal-cutting tool.
- Two of the most inexpensive plastic ballpoint pens that you can find. You can recycle a couple of old ones if you like.
- Two pieces of the kind of plaster that you put on a cut finger.
- This is the hardest part: One nice man or a woman who has strong hands.

Take one of the metal coat hangers and cut it in two places with the pliers. If like me, you don't have strong hands, this is where your man-friend or strong woman will come in useful. The first cut should be at the end of the straight bit at the bottom, before it begins to curve upwards. The second is at the upper end of the short arm, before it bends and starts to join the twirly bit at the top that forms the hook. If you now straighten the hanger out a bit, you will have an "L" shaped object that has one long end and one short end, with a 90 degree angle between the two sides. If you can remember back to your school days, this is like the two sides of a right-angled triangle with the hypotenuse missing.

Now do the same with the second hanger.

Take the pens and pull the buttons off from their ends; use the pliers to pull the inky working part of the pens out, and throw all these pieces away. You now have two plastic tubes or sleeves and you should insert the short arms of the wire hanger pieces into the pen sleeves.

I now suggest that you stick the pieces of plaster on the ends of the rods as a precaution, in case you accidentally stab yourself with the rods or stick them into someone's eyes. As a more attractive alternative to plasters, you could glue small wooden beads onto the ends of the rods. As I said before, the health and legal risk is yours, so take care when making or using the rods.

### Exercises: Using your rods

Open your chakras and pick up your rods. Hold the plastic sleeves without letting your fingers touch any part of the metal hangers. Swing the rods around gently for a moment to check that they move around easily. The difference in the diameter of the metal rod and the hole in the sleeve means that they should swing around freely.

Hold the rods out in front of you with your hands at a distance of about ten to twelve inches from your body and with your hands about eight inches apart. Beginners tend to clutch the rods too close to their bodies and too close to each other; this makes them difficult to use, so don't be afraid of stretching out and using a bit of space.

Now raise and lower the ends of the rods until you feel that you have enough control over them to stop them swinging from side to side, but not so much that gravity pulls them down and holds them in place. This takes a little practice. It is also worth holding the handles lightly, rather than clutching them for grim death.

Next, think "yes" and keep on thinking of the word "yes" until something happens. After a short while, the rods may start to tremble, then they will slowly start to move. The rods usually cross - but they may part, or one rod may swing across while the other one swings outward. Whatever the rods do will be your "yes", and you should be able to replicate the same action every time you think "yes".

Now start again, but this time, think "no". The chances are that the rods crossed when you thought "yes" and that they will swing apart when you think "no", but they may do something different. The action of the rods is immaterial, as long as you end up with one movement that is your "yes" and another for your "no".

Once you have got this far, you will be able to form any kind of question in your mind and get an answer. The question has to be formed in such a way that a straightforward "yes" or "no" answer can be obtained. Such questions as, "Should I date Joe or Steve?" will get you nowhere. You need to ask whether you should date Joe, and see what answer you get - then try the same thing for Steve. The rods might tell you to date Joe or Steve, or both of them, or neither of them - but they will give you an answer.

### *Directions*

Once you have the basics under your belt, here is a wonderful thing to try. Treat yourself to an inexpensive compass - the kind of thing that hikers and boy and girl scouts use to find their way around. Put the compass down without looking at it. Do not align it to north or try to discover in which direction you are facing. Take your rods and hold them out in the usual way and then very slowly turn yourself around and around, holding the rods out in front of you. While doing this; mentally ask to be shown where the four points of the compass are located.

The rods are metal, so a combination of the earth's magnetism and your psychic mind will do the trick. The rods will probably cross when you reach each compass point. Even if they don't do this at first, they will certainly tremble and act in a peculiar way or appear to cling to each of the compass points. You may only be able to pick up a north/south or east/west axis at first (for some reason the east/west axis is often the easiest for a beginner to find). Soon, you will be able to pick up all four compass points and perhaps even find ways of working out which is which. Whatever results you get, check them with your compass.

Once you have perfected the dowsing technique, you can look for water pipes under the ground, find the nearest petrol station when you need one, find your way home or look for something that you have mislaid. After a while, you will probably find many different uses for this strange skill. You may even be able to find water in the desert, or to strike oil in your own back yard!

### *The three failures*

I have taught many different kinds of people how to use dowsing rods, and in all my years, I have only come across three people who couldn't do it. All three were men. Two of them had such closed minds that they simply refused to believe that the rods would work. Nobody suggests that psychic work is a matter of blind faith and belief, but we do know that even such a basic form of psychic exercise as this needs an open mind. If someone is really determined that something won't work for them, then it won't. The third was a rather sad case.

George's wife, Milly, had died of cancer a couple of years earlier, and Milly had been given quite a bit of spiritual healing before her death. George argued that the fact that Milly had died proved that spiritual healing didn't work, and that nothing else of the kind could possibly work either. As it happened, poor George had completely missed the point of spiritual healing. A healer cannot prevent a person from dying if the universe says that it is that person's time to go, but spiritual healing will reduce pain and mental anguish. The healers had not explained this to George, but when I pointed it out to him, he agreed that this had definitely been the case with Milly, that she had become easier in her mind and her pain had eased as a result of the healing.

### *Pendulum dowsing*

Pendulums are not expensive to buy. You can treat yourself to a crystal pendulum on a chain, a wooden one, or any kind of pendulum that you fancy. If you don't want to buy one, you can adapt a necklace that has a pendant on it, thread a small stone that has a hole in it onto some stout thread, or in an emergency you can even use a fairly heavy bodkin-type needle and some thread. You will need a length of thin chain or thread that is long enough to dangle, but not so long that it is hard to handle. No more than twelve inches should do the trick. You can hold the pendulum in either hand, and you may wish to experiment to see if it works better with one hand than the other.

### *Exercises: Using your pendulum*

Open your chakras and then take hold of the pendulum, allowing about six or seven inches of chain or thread and the pendant to dangle down. Dangle the pendulum a few inches above the palm of your other hand, then think "yes" and keep on thinking "yes" until something happens.

The pendulum may move back and forth, from side to side or in a circle. It may swing wildly or it may only move a little. Whatever movement you get is your "yes", and you can check this by trying the experiment again later. Once you have found your "yes", do the same thing again to find your "no". Now you can use your pendulum to answer questions that require a positive or negative reply.

Here are a couple more experiments that you can try. Ask your pendulum to pick up the chakras that are located in each of your fingertips and then dangle the pendulum over each fingertip. You should find that the pendulum reverses its direction, or changes its action to a back and forth motion over different fingertips.

Ask an acquaintance to draw a rough outline of his house without marking which room is which. Dowse over the illustration, asking the pendulum to find the kitchen or some other room that you choose to search for. It will react once you are over the part of the house that you have asked the pendulum to identify. Try to find a second type of room, and then try asking for specific things, such as the position of the fridge, television, dog's kennel or anything else that you fancy.

You may find while doing these experiments that you start to get visions of the house in your mind's eye. Check your findings with your friend by describing what you see, because the chances are that you will be right. This will be a bigger surprise to you than it will be to your friend.

If you mislay something, your pendulum will lead you to the place where you left it, and you can use this with a design of your office, car or any other place that you wish to search. If visions start to come while you are working with the pendulum - just let them. If you are dowsing over a friend's house or workplace, describe anything that you see in your mind's eye and ask your pal to give you some feedback.

Ask a friend to think about someone who has an ailment or some part of their body that is not functioning properly. Then ask him to draw an image of the person. Your buddy doesn't need to be an artist, because any kind of childish drawing will do - even a stick figure will work. He just needs to concentrate on the person while he draws.

Now take your pendulum and start at the top of the drawing, slowly moving the pendulum from side to side, gradually moving down the illustration. Do it a couple more times if necessary to corroborate your results. You may find that the pendulum becomes active when it reaches the part of the body that is out of balance. Alternatively, it may stick to that part of the body as if it is drawn to it, and it may feel as though it doesn't want to move away from the area. Check your findings with your friend.

While doing this, you may find yourself picking up an image of the sick person in your head. You may feel that a particular part of the body in the picture is trying to get your attention or to climb into your mind in some way. Allow yourself be drawn into the clairsentience (feeling psychically) and then check your findings with your friend. You may get the distinct impression of a particular kind of ailment, and you may even start to pick up information on when or how it started and its possible prognosis.

You may feel a kind of vague discomfort in your own body. If this happens, once you have finished your experiment, sit quietly for a while and imagine cool clear water coming down from the universe, entering the top of your head and coursing through every part of your body and out through your extremities. There is little chance of you "catching" the sick person's illness, but you could end up feeling uncomfortable for a while, and there is no need to put up with that for long.

### *Ley lines*

There is a belief that parts of the world are linked by something called ley lines. The southern part of Britain has a long chain of ancient places that seem to be linked in a spiritual manner, these being Glastonbury Tor, Wells Cathedral, Avebury, Salisbury Cathedral, Silbury Hill, Stone Henge and even the Pilgrims route to Canterbury. It is said that a particularly powerful ley line links these places. It is also believed that smaller ley lines occur or even cross each other at ancient fords, bridges and major crossing places of all kinds. Apparently there is a strong ley line by the entrance to Westminster tube station in London, close by Westminster Bridge, the Houses of Parliament and almost on top of what was once Westminster Palace. Smaller ley lines or energy lines can even turn up in people's houses, schools, offices, hospitals, workshops and just about everywhere else.

Some of these are considered to be positive ley lines and others negative ley lines. It is possible that the ancient people who worked out some of the principles of Feng Shui picked up these kinds of energies. Feng Shui specialists tell us that sitting or sleeping under a beam is bad for us, as is living in a house that has a straight hallway, and worse still, with doors at either end that are in line with one another. The Feng Shui expert will show us how to "break up" these influences by dangling things from a beam or by draping cloth around it, and by placing rounded tables, floor mats and other such objects into a straight hallway.

Leaving the subject of Feng Shui for the moment and returning to ley lines, take your rods or pendulum and walk slowly backwards and forwards across your room. Mentally ask if there is a positive ley line present. If your dowsing tools give you a reaction in a certain area, walk back and forth over it several times until you are sure that you are getting the right reading. Now do the same for negative ley lines. You may not find any kind of ley line in the area you are exploring, but don't put this down to your ineptitude, it is just that there may be no lines in that location. If you or anyone you know feels uncomfortable in a particular part of a room for no logical reason, test it out for a negative ley line and see what comes up. There may be some other reason for your friend's dislike of a particular area - it might even be haunted! Well, we will look into ghost busting later in this book, and you may wish to use your dowsing rods or pendulum for that too.

Whatever kind of dowsing you perform, do remember to close your chakras when you have finished.

### *Geophysics and psychic archeology*

Depending upon your own particular form of psychism, receptiveness, sensitivity and so on, you may eventually be able to dowse without using any tools at all. If you do find a ley line, try putting your tools aside and walking backwards and forwards over an area, as though you were crossing and re-crossing a path. See if you can feel any vague pressure on your body, rather as though the air in that area is slightly thicker than it is elsewhere. Once you have become accustomed to this feeling of pressure, you will be able to use it for other purposes. The following story will show you what I mean.

### *A true story*

One day, my friend Jonathan Dee and I decided to look around the ruins of Nonesuch house, in Nonesuch Park in Cheam in Surrey, which we knew had connections with Henry the Eighth and Anne Boleyn. At the back of the park were the foundations of part of the original house. For some reason, we decided to discover where the entrance to the house had originally been, so we walked back and forth along the wooded path that led to the ruins, with our chakras open and focusing on any possible change in the air around our bodies. We both felt a peculiar sense of pressure in one particular spot, and when we scratched away some of the earthen path and we found a line of ancient brickwork running across it that marked the position of the entrance.

### *Fingertip dowsing and house-hunting*

When you get used to dowsing, you will be able to dowse over an illustration or a map with your fingertips. You can try the experiment that I described earlier with the picture of the layout of a friend's house or the illustration of a sick person and see if your fingertips react. Just focus on what it is that you are looking for and you may feel heat at the spot or you may feel that the air in that area appears to be thicker than it is elsewhere.

### *Map dowsing*

When Jan and I decided to move away from London, we surfed the Internet to see what houses were available in different areas of the country. We eventually boiled our choices down to three completely different locations around Britain. I dowsed over a map of Britain by drifting my fingertips over it to see which route would be ours. I felt my fingertips warming up all along a wide swathe of country that led to the southwest. We then looked into various locations all around the country by sending off requests to local real estate agencies. Eventually, we came to the conclusion that we should take a trip and look for possibilities to the south west of England. After viewing a few houses, we ended up happily living in the city of Plymouth in Devon, at the end of the route that had felt like warm treacle to my fingertips.

# 8

## Using the Tarot for Psychic Purposes

In earlier years, psychic societies almost forbade the use of Tarot cards and other such tools, and their members believed that those who used them were of a lower order. This has changed now, and even the Spiritualist Associations agree that Tarot has its uses. You may remember the story of Andrew Morton who was trained by the CIA. He says in his book that there were some Tarot readers in his department, but that he didn't think much of them, because his own psychism was of a higher order than theirs was. Well, Mr. Morton was the first to say that his particular gift almost destroyed his life, so perhaps those of us who use such tools are not so silly after all.

You may find using the Tarot cards a good way of opening your inner eye to the psychic world. When it comes to psychic matters, you must find your own truth, and the opinions of others should not be allowed to influence you. Neither should you in your turn censure anybody who works in a different way to you.

If you feel like using Tarot cards, go ahead and do so, because you will find that they lead you towards the psychic world in their own strange and subtle manner. There are hundreds of books on the market that will show you how to read Tarot cards, and I have written several of them myself. Buy books by several different authors, because each person uses slightly different interpretations for the cards, and it is a good idea to broaden your knowledge rather than to follow just one author's methods. There are also many different kinds of Tarot cards on the market. For the moment, use a standard deck like the Universal Tarot, the Rider Waite Tarot or the Hanson Roberts deck. If you fall in love with other types of cards, keep them, to use later when you are comfortable with the meanings of the Tarot cards and when your ESP has developed.

Most people find that the pictures on the cards help their intuition, but some find that these get in their way. If you are one of those people, buy the less illustrated kind of card, or even teach yourself to use playing cards instead. As usual with psychic matters, what works for you is right for you.

There are some specialist shops that keep several decks aside as samples to show customers what the cards inside the packages look like, but in most cases the boxes of cards are sealed and you cannot see what is inside. Try looking on the Internet, because those who sell Tarot cards display their wares there. Once you have found what you want, you can order your cards over the 'net, or to go to a shop and buy them.

You can prepare a new deck of cards by meditating while you hold them in your hands, and you can ask the universe to bless them and to make them work for you. If you want to take this further, or to "cleanse" an old deck, hold the cards and call down light from the universe, surrounding the cards with the light for a while.

### *To learn or not to learn*

You can learn the meaning of each card by heart, or you can use the illustrations on the cards purely to give you an impression of what is going on in a person's life, and you can also use a mixture of both methods. There is something to be said for learning the meaning of the cards, because you will draw an occasional psychic blank when giving a reading, and when this happens you can always fall back on their textbook meanings. On the other hand, you must not allow the standard meanings to cloud or overshadow any feelings that you get while giving a reading.

A particular image on a card may catch your attention during a reading, and it may send a message to you in a way that has never happened before. If you find a thought or feeling coming into your head, leave the standard meaning of the card behind and go with the flow - or add your own impressions to the standard meaning. If you get any gut feeling, mental impression or stray thought coming through, do let them out. Your intuition is unlikely to be wrong, and the more you use it the more it will grow in strength and confidence.

The same thing applies to the feeling you get when you lay out a spread of cards. The combination of cards may present an instant picture of what is happening in your questioner's life, and occasionally this may have little to do with the actual meanings of each individual card in the layout. The message here is to use the Tarot as an easy means of linking you to what is going on in your client's life, while it also wedges open the door to your own ESP. You may find that there are times when you hardly read the cards at all, merely using them to jump-start your intuition, but there will also be times when you need to fall back on them.

If you reach a point where you find that the cards are getting in your way and that you are happier without them, leave them alone. However, you may be glad of them when you have an off day, or when you want confirmation of some mental impression that you are getting. Having said all the above, your own intuition is always your best guide. If you get a feeling about the person for whom you are reading, go with it, because it will be right.

Some people like to hold an object that belongs to their client while giving a reading, as a psychometric way of tuning in to the person. Others ask their clients to put their hands on a crystal ball for a few moments before the reading, and then the reader glances at the ball and picks up messages from within it or in their mind's eye. There are many methods of reading Tarot (or Runes or anything else of the kind) and you must use the one that works best for you.

### Beating the magicians

If you are used to reading any kind of cards, be they Tarot, playing cards, Rune cards, I Ching cards, Dakini cards or anything else at all, try this experiment. Take your cards and shuffle them well, then pick several cards from the deck without looking at them and place them face downward on the table. If you wish, you can ask someone else to do this for you. Then pass your hand slowly over each card and try to obtain an impression of what it is telling you. You may pick up a picture in your mind of the image that is on the other side of the card, or you may pick up the story that the particular group of cards has to tell you. Once you have noted down what you think you feel about them, turn the cards over. You may be surprised by how close you can get to the story written in the cards.

### A true story

I could tell you enough stories about Tarot readings to fill ten books, but let me illustrate the point with just one. In the past, I earned my living by giving readings, and I saw many clients during the course of each week. Most of them came and went without leaving an impression, but the following is one of many stories that remained in my memory.

### Paula

Paula was a small, dark haired, rather intense young woman who had come to me for readings on several occasions. Her life wasn't bad, but it had no real meaning or purpose - and more to the point, there was no man in her life. One day, she came for a reading, and when I laid the cards out they shrieked that her life was about to change in a major way. I remember that all four of the Aces, the Fool card and the Wheel of Fortune turned up in the first spread that I laid out, and this alerted me to the fact that something outstanding was about to happen in Paula's life. A subsequent spread gave me the impression that she would travel to a hot country, have many interesting and uplifting happenings there and that she would find her Prince Charming. My intuition told me that Paula's life was about to change quite radically. I also felt that she should go along with any opportunities that turned up and to see where they led her. This reading mystified Paula, but she knew that the cards (and my intuition) were rarely wrong, so she accepted it.

About a year later, Paula turned up again. It happened that some few weeks after her reading, she had seen an advertisement in a magazine for people to work as volunteers in the Sudan in Africa. Paula had no ties, so she threw up her boring office job, rented out her apartment and took off to the Sudan. She worked as a nursing assistant to those who were starving and sick. The work fulfilled her, and she started a worthwhile relationship with a doctor who she met there. After a few years of such work, both came back to Britain and lived happily ever after.

This kind of reading is partly guided partly by the Tarot and partly by the Reader's natural intuition. Not every psychic can just pick up things by being with a person, so the Tarot is often a good way of jump-starting the psychic energies.

# 9

## Seeing and Feeling the Aura

Those who regularly see auras are pretty rare specimens even among psychics, so if you cannot see an aura for looking, don't be disappointed - though you may actually see auras from time to time without really being aware of it. Next time you watch someone who is teaching, talking in an animated way or in some other way "giving out" while they are talking, you may notice a narrow band of fuzzy light around them. You may even realize that you have been seeing this band of light all your life, although it is only now that I point it out to you that you become aware of the phenomenon.

### *Exercises for seeing an aura*

Try looking at any living thing: a person, an animal or a growing plant, and see if you can spot this auric outline. It is best to allow your eyes to become unfocused and to stare at it rather vaguely. Even if you have no luck with this, try the following experiment.

- Ask a friend to sit or stand against a plain background.
- Stare at your friend for a few moments and allow your eyes to drift slightly out of focus.
- Close your eyes and notice the grayish shape of your friend temporarily imprinted on your retina.
- Open your eyes again and look at your friend once more. Do this for a few moments.

- Now close your eyes again and concentrate on what is going on around the gray figure. You will start to see lights and colors swirling around it.
- When you open your eyes again, you may still see something of this aura hanging around the person, but you may always find it easier to see with your "third eye" rather than with your real eyes.

Try this again with the same friend or with another one, but this time when you see the aura, ask several different friends to think of things that make them happy, sad, angry, worried, hopeful, contented, excited, amused and so on. See if you can spot changes in the shape or colors in the aura.

You may have this experience when meditating alone, and this time it is something from your own aura that you will see.

### *The color code*

There are various interpretations for the colors that you will see in the aura. If you become an accomplished aura reader, you will build up your own ideas of what the colors mean, based on your own experience. You may discover that whenever you see a certain shade in the aura, the person is looking for love, or is worried about children, money, health and so on.

However, here are some pretty standard interpretations that will give you something to go on until you have developed your own ideas:

- Red indicates strong feelings, such as passion and anger. We "see red" when we are angry.
- All shades of pink represent love and affection. They can also indicate being "in the pink", that is healthy and happy.
- Orange signifies energy and good health.
- Yellow not only symbolizes energy and health, but also intelligence and teaching ability.

- Green indicates affection and anything to do with money or material resources, but remember the old saying that someone can be "green with envy".
- Brown is definitely a money and resource color, but it also suggests retreat and reflection, as in a "brown study".
- Pale blue or turquoise represent healing ability and also a talent for communication.
- Dark blue suggests teaching ability and definite talent for communication. Remember all those songs about "feeling blue" - so perhaps it can also mean being unhappy and depressed about love.
- Lilac, lavender, mauve, purple or white will show up when a person is doing spiritual work, such as channeling or healing.

### *Feeling the aura*

Even if you cannot see an aura, most people find it easy to feel an aura, so try the following:

- Open your chakras and put your hands together in front of you.
- Slowly pull them apart until there is a gap of about eighteen inches between your palms.
- Very slowly bring your hands back together again. Concentrate on what you feel as your hands move closer to each other, because there will be a point where the air feels thick between your hands. This may feel as though you are pressing on the contents of an invisible balloon, to the point where you can almost bounce your hands on this invisible pressure.
- Do the same thing several times, until you are certain that you are feeling something.

This feeling of pressure may come when your hands are about a foot apart, six inches apart or really quite close to each other. Whatever the distance, what you are feeling is the aura of one hand meeting that of the other. The depth of the aura will depend upon your state of mind and your state of health, because it tends to shrink when a person is ill or unhappy.

If you try this with no success, it may be that you are tired, off-color or you may have recently eaten a large meal. If you are unhappy or if you are shielding yourself from someone else's bad behavior, your aura will pull into itself and there will be little or nothing to feel. In these cases, leave the experiment for the time being and try again another day.

If you feel bad, it is always worth strengthening your aura by imagining yourself encased in a shiny coat of armor. Even if you still don't feel much after doing this, it will help to protect you.

### *Enlisting the help of others*

Ask someone to pass his or her hand, slowly, back and forth over yours at a distance of an inch or two, and see what you can feel, then do the same for your friend. We all have a field of static electricity surrounding us, so if you try rubbing your hand up and down the back of someone's forearm without touching it, the hairs on his arm will stand up.

Try the same thing with your feet, so that you are sending your aura and feeling his through his shoes and socks. This time there should be no direct connection with the body's static electricity. Did you and your friend feel any sensation, such as tingling, friction, heat, cold or any other kind of feeling? When I do this to people, they tell me that they can feel intense heat and sometimes also tingling, despite the fact that my hands are usually very cool to the touch.

Ask your friend to turn around so that his back is towards you, so that he cannot see what you are doing. Then pass your hands over his back in a criss-cross manner, at a distance of about two inches and ask him to report anything that he feels. Then ask your friend to do the same thing to you. You or your friend may even start to fall backwards towards the hand movements.

Now ask your friend to stand with his back to you, and gently place your hand on his back. Send him some really kind and healing thoughts, and see if he gets a good feeling from this. Now ask him to do the same for you.

If you have a few friends who are willing to be guinea pigs, you should ask them to stand in a row, several feet from you and facing you. Then concentrate on pushing your aura out to a certain point in front of them. Ask them to walk very slowly towards you and to stop when they feel something. You could issue your friends with dowsing rods and ask them to focus on finding the edge of your aura; the rods will react when they meet it. Try sending out loving thoughts, healing thoughts and even sexy ones via your aura, and see which ones your friends can detect.

The following is an exercise that I often use towards the end of my psychic demonstrations, and it always gets a good laugh. I have to thank my mischievous friend, Barbara Ellen, for this one:

Find a friend of the opposite sex to yourself, or the same sex if you and your pals happen to be gay. If you have a few more friends who can act as an audience to this exercise, so much the better. Both you and your friend will need to open your chakras before trying this. Give your friend a pair of dowsing rods to hold and ask him to stand across the room from you with his back turned towards you, while he holds the rods out in front of himself. Stand back to back with your friend, and while he stands still, you should walk slowly away from him, almost as if you were dueling with pistols at dawn. Do this as silently as you can. After a few paces, turn and face your friend's back and send him the sexiest thought you can dream up, while pushing your aura towards your friend as hard as you can. Keep this up until the rods or pendulum react. The reaction is likely to be fast - and the rods may move quite violently!

The reason that I suggest sending a sexy thought is that sex is a powerful energy that will get through to most people. You could achieve the same thing by sending bad vibes and hateful thoughts, but this will stick with your friend afterwards, making him feel uncomfortable or even unwell.

If you are really cheeky, next time you see someone that you fancy, try quietly sending a sexy thought out in your aura and see if it does anything to help your cause. Naughty, I know. But as long as the person is available and you mean no harm, it should be all right. Never send bad vibes, even if you feel them to be justified, because these will always bounce back on you.

If you feel that someone else is sending you bad vibes - not necessarily psychic ones, but such things as dislike, jealousy and animosity - or that they are taking out their bad mood on you, there are ways of protecting yourself and of deflecting such vibes. We will look into this in the chapter on psychic self-defense.

## *Aura energies*

We all know what it feels like to walk into a room where people have been fighting or where someone is unhappy. To some extent, scraps of the aura that people leave behind can hang around a place after the sad or unpleasant events have taken place. This accounts for the uncomfortable sensations, unhappiness or, alternatively, happy vibes that buildings hold within them.

I have a photograph that was taken years ago when I was giving a psychic reading, which shows a strange blob of light hanging about three feet above my head, when there was no reason for such a light to appear in this photo. I kept an open mind about this until recently, when a very spiritual friend showed me an almost identical photo that was taken while he was giving a reading. My photo was taken in 1982, my friend's photo was taken in 1995, and they were taken at completely separate venues with different cameras. A trick of the light? A faulty film? But perhaps this was the presence of "spirit", or possibly something weird that our auras were shooting out into the atmosphere.

## *A tragic story*

Some years ago, my cousin Brian telephoned me and he sounded very upset. He told me that he had been driving slowly down a busy road when his attention was drawn to a woman walking along the sidewalk (pavement to British readers). He described seeing a gray, cobwebby aura hanging around her head and shoulders. Before I could stop myself, I commented that the woman would soon be dead - if she wasn't already. Brian said that I was quite right. Apparently he had driven past her and then watched a horror story unfold in his rear-view mirror. The woman couldn't have been thinking what she was doing, because Brian saw her stepping out into the traffic, being hit by a truck and being sent sky-high by the impact.

Brian was naturally very disturbed at having witnessed this woman's death, but he was even more disturbed by having had his attention drawn to the "death aura" that he had seen immediately before the event. I reassured him that this was normal among psychics. The only reason that he hadn't witnessed it before was because he hadn't tried to develop his natural gifts, but this event was so strong that he couldn't help picking it up.

# 10

# Clairvoyance, Clairaudience and Clairsentience

### *Terminology*

There are many skills that come under the general umbrella of clairvoyance and that describe a variety of techniques. The obvious idea is of being able to see things remotely. A clairvoyant may see occurrences that have already happened, or events that are still somewhere out there in the future. He may be able to see a person's home, office, hotel room or any number of locations at a distance. Many people refer to mediumship and channeling as clairvoyance. In addition, the channeler may hear and feel certain happenings. Various areas blend together here, so the whole business covers a great deal of ground. We must start somewhere though, so here are some strict definitions of the three "clairs".

### *Clairvoyance*

A clairvoyant sees things that are not immediately apparent. The word "clairvoyance" means clear seeing, but in my experience what one sees is anything but clear, and that seeing shadows might be a better way of expressing this.

Most clairvoyants see pictures in their heads, as a kind of vague mental impression, and this is often backed up by a positive feeling that what they are seeing is right. The easiest way that I can explain this is to ask you to think back to an event that occurred recently and bring it to mind. You will see what the place looked like in your mind's eye and you will find it easy to describe to your friend. You will be able to tell him what the people there were wearing, and what they said and did. The somewhat disjointed manner in which you can recall and describe an event is very much like the kind of mental impression that is received and then passed on to a client by a clairvoyant.

## Clairaudience

A clairaudient hears voices or sounds. In my experience, there are fewer people who regularly receive messages by clairaudience than by clairvoyance or clairsentience, although any psychic can receive an occasional clairaudient message. Sometimes the voices or sounds are like a vague background noise that comes from behind the clairaudient's head. Sometimes they are surprisingly loud, as though someone had come up behind the clairaudient and put his mouth close to this ear, loudly whispering a message.

## Clairsentience

Clairsentience is the most common of all these phenomena and many perfectly ordinary people have clairsentient experiences. Clairsentience means the ability to sense or feel things. This is more than just the kind of intuition that kicks in when we feel that something isn't right. Examples of clairsentience might be of smelling perfume when there is nobody present and no reason for the smell to be there, or it can feel as though there is something brushing past us. Emotions pass themselves through a clairsentient person, so he can tap into what others feel.

When a psychic or medium is trying to pick things up, he will focus his whole body while tuning in. Rather than the stereotypical image of a medium sitting in a trance, many mediums pace back and forth like a caged animal while working, so that they can pick things up with their bodies as well as with their minds.

## *Exercise - getting something through*

It is not easy for me to dream up an exercise for you to try here, and you will probably have more success with psychometry, but you can try the following idea:

Open your chakras and focus your mind on someone who you know, but whom you don't know very much about. Walk slowly back and forth and see if you can feel something in the atmosphere that tells you something about the person's state of mind. Tune in to the emotional atmosphere around the person and see what you feel. It is not at all easy for me to describe this because we are in the misty, shadowy realm of feelings and of things that aren't evident and obvious. Give it a try, and if possible ask the person if anything that you felt, saw, heard, smelled, tasted or just "knew" made any kind of connection.

## *Feeling a signature*

As I said before, the different ways of working blend into each other, so the following story is really about a form of psychometry, although it can also be deemed clairvoyance.

I once worked as secretary to an international businessman called Les. Like many top business people, he was a very intuitive man. In those days, most long distance negotiations were initially conducted by telex, in much the same way that we use email today. However, it was normal for any agreement to be followed up by a signed letter. Even when this was not the case, Les always insisted on being sent such a letter and he would not take action until he had received it. Of course, it is good business practice to wait for a signed document, but that was not the point here. Once the letter arrived, Les would put his thumb on the signature and tune into the intentions of the sender. That way, he avoided being stitched into deals that would not be in his favor!

You can try this for yourself by using a fairly unimportant document. If you find that it works for you, it will become an invaluable (if rather unusual) way of keeping ahead of the business game!

## Large-scale events

There are people who love to dramatize themselves. I once had a friend whom I shall call Alison. Alison didn't work in the psychic field, but she loved being the center of attention, and she used every means to achieve this. One of her "things" was dreaming of air crashes. Every time there was an air crash, she swore that she had dreamed about it a couple of weeks before. Her dramatics might have been more convincing if she told people of the air disasters before they happened. Even so, there are so many air accidents in large and small craft that sooner or later she would definitely have been able to say that she had predicted one of them.

## Didn't you see it coming?

Civilians laugh at psychics when they are taken by surprise at some disaster or other, but if we were tuned into every earthquake, flood, bush fire, volcano, train crash or other disaster in the world before it happened, we would soon inhabit a padded cell!

Having said that, the dreadful atrocity at the Twin Towers of the World Trade Center was in a league of its own. Many psychics everywhere picked it up and many actually phoned the police, the FBI and the White House to warn them. Two days before the event, I had a strange science-fiction type of dream in which I saw some kind of craft docking in the upper level of a tall building, and then I saw a second one doing the same in an adjacent building. I only made the connection with the Twin Towers after the event, as the dream gave no clues as to the event's significance, date, location, or even country. Several friends phoned to tell me that they had dreamed of the disaster or that they had received a psychic "flash" about it. This is not surprising, as just about every sensitive person in the western world must have felt this one coming.

Another thing that will drive you nuts is when something goes wrong in your own life and some wag laughs and asks why you didn't see it coming. You can't see everything coming; but even when you do, what are you supposed to do about it? I recently had the feeling that something to do with our office communications systems was likely to go wrong, but I couldn't pick up on exactly what this would be. Was I supposed to replace our telephone system, computers, scanners, printers and even our vehicle on the strength of this? A few days later, one of our computers died a death, and before we could get this replaced and re-install all its software programs onto a new machine, a second computer went down and spent days in the menders. Having foreknowledge is all very well, but it doesn't always help - and ordinary people can't see how frustrating that can be!

### *Timing of events*

The hardest thing for a professional psychic to do is to tell a client when something is going to happen. The spirit world doesn't seem to recognize time in the way that we do, so a message can be perfectly true, although it may be many years before the event comes about. There is one trick that you can try, which works like this.

Imagine a calendar and try to see which month is at the top of it. Ask the calendar to keep on tearing off pages until the right month for the predicted event shows up. If you are really lucky, one of the days of the month will start to flash on and off, change color or stand out on the calendar. Having said this, the fact is that astrology is a far better tool than psychism when it comes to timing events.

# 11

## Psychometry

Psychometry is the art of holding an object such as a wristwatch or a piece of jewelry in one's hand and picking up an impression from it. This is commonly used as a form of training in psychic or spiritual groups. The real reason for doing this is to feel the history of the object itself, but nobody is interested in the travels of a ring or a wristwatch, so naturally, we tune into the history of the person who has worn the watch. Anybody who does this will ask their client to give them something that has never been owned or worn by anybody else, because multiple ownership confuses the images and feelings that the clairvoyant is trying to pick up.

### *An exercise in psychometry*

Gather some friends around and ask them to bring pieces of jewelry and wristwatches with them. The objects may belong to your friends or to people who they know. Equip yourself with a small basket or bowl. Each person should put an object into the basket. When they have done so, they should pass the basket around so that each person can take something out of it. The participants should then hold the objects and try to tune into the emotions, stories and visions that might come from the object. If you haven't opened your chakras or asked your guide for help, do so now.

The first thing that is likely to come is any emotion that is held within the object. Your pals will soon start to pick up on feelings of happiness, unhappiness, frustration, anger and so on. They may soon be able to tune into the personality of the object's owner. After several practice sessions, they may be able to pick up on specific areas of life, such as a relationship, a job, a journey, a health matter, family problems and perhaps joy and excitement due to some specific event. Some group members may start to see pictures or get messages from beyond the grave, or they may pick up on a future event. Anything can happen.

Some professional clairvoyants bump start their readings by asking their clients to put their hands on a crystal ball for a few moments. The clairvoyant then takes the ball and holds it, picking up the images and feelings from the client in that way. I have seen one clairvoyant using a large stone for this purpose.

### *Photograph and letter psychometry*

It is possible to make a link via photographs or hand-written letters. Take the photo or letter, don't look at it but simply hold it lightly between the palms of your hands. You may feel the paper become warm or tingly, or you may feel nothing special. Mentally ask your spirit guides to show you something about the person or situation. Clouds or mist may appear in front of your eyes, and then feelings, visions or perhaps sounds should start to come in. You will feel as though you are trying to see, feel and hear something that is very far away, but the images will become sharper and more detailed if you give yourself time.

### *Psychometry can be hot stuff*

Many years ago, while I was looking into all things psychic, I visited a psychic reader who asked me to bring along objects for her to use as a link. She suggested that I bring my own things and also things that belonged to any people about whom I wanted to hear. You may remember me talking about my powerful boss, Les, in a previous chapter? Well, Les was happy for me to experiment on him, so I took his watch along for the ride.

Once the psychic had gone through my store of objects, I handed over the watch. Before taking it, she asked me to tell her under which sign of the zodiac the watch's owner was born. I told her that he was a Libran and she said that he must be something of a wimp, as Libra is not a strong sign. I didn't bother telling this opinionated psychic that I was an astrologer, and neither did I point out that a person with a Sun, Mercury, and Mars conjunction in the first house was never going to be any kind of wimp! I just watched and waited while she took the watch in her hand. To my amusement, she almost dropped it on the floor! She had picked up the power and dominance of my boss's personality, and she told me afterwards that the watch had actually felt red-hot!

# 12

## Proof of Survival

The basic purpose of spiritualism and the spiritualist movement is "proof of survival". This means proof that the soul carries on after the physical body has died. There are spiritualist churches and spiritualist centers. Some churches have a Christian bias, but others do not. In either case, the service usually starts with an opening prayer and a rather pleasant hymn or two, and then the main part of the service or event commences. A medium stands in front of the congregation or audience and passes messages on to various members from relatives who have died. The messages may be very mundane, but they usually mean something to the recipient. Even when they don't, the chances are that the recipient will go home, look into it and discover that the messages were true. An example may be something along the lines of, "The day your father and I were married was very wet, and I went down the aisle with soaking shoes."

Messages may be mundane or profound, but they often bring comfort the bereaved. Many of those who have passed over are keen to tell their loved ones that they are now out of pain, no longer crippled with arthritis or old and weary, and that they are happy to be where they are.

Sometimes a message can be amusing. I have seen stuffy people give a medium a hard time for making the audience laugh. The etiquette of these meetings doesn't usually allow for the recipient to question the medium or to ask for more information, so the experience is interesting, but it can be somewhat limited.

## *Private sittings*

Those who work in the spiritualist movement often give their time and energies free of charge, but they also have to live - and this can cause confusion. Many of those who work in this field have a normal job that brings in the money that they need, but some rely on private clients for an income. Such people may work at home and they may also work at psychic fairs and so on. The work that they do may be similar to that which is carried out in a spiritualist center, so the confusion between the medium or healer's free work and his paid work can lead to undue criticism or disapproval. Everybody needs to live, and the self-righteous accuser will be sure to have some kind of income or living of his own. If a psychic or healer chooses to earn money by giving private sittings, then good luck to him. There will certainly be no shortage of clients who understand the system and who are only too glad to pay.

As I said earlier, there is a limit to what is done and what can be done in a public arena. Many people go on to book a private sitting with the medium so that they can go into things more deeply. Also, not everyone can bear to wash their family linen in public.

## *The flying dessert*

As I said, some messages are amusing, and this can be quite disconcerting to the poor medium who has to pass them on. The following story is a real life example of this in action.

Betty Nugent gives private sittings for clients. On one occasion, she was dealing with a middle-aged female who had not told Betty the purpose of her visit. It later transpired that the woman was hoping to receive a message from her much-loved mother who had recently passed over. The opening salvo came when Betty received a message that a boy called Jim had once thrown a plate of jelly (jello) and ice cream into her client's face. Betty was just beginning to cope with having to pass on this message without laughing when her client suddenly burst into tears. Betty dug out a box of tissues and poured the client a glass of water. Once the poor woman had composed herself, she told Betty that this event had taken place over fifty years previously at her fifth birthday party. The only person who could possibly have known about it was her mother, because it was she who had mopped up the dessert and comforted the crying birthday girl. The message proved to the client that it was indeed her mother who was talking to her. This, plus some more usual types of messages that followed, gave the client the emotional release and comfort that she needed.

Those who know nothing of spiritual work like to accuse mediums of telling clients stuff that is so obvious that any person could have spewed it out - but this story proves just how wrong this assumption is. No medium takes the trouble to research a client for fraudulent purposes. It would be far too difficult and too time consuming, and in view of the pitiful amount of money that a medium can expect to be paid for a sitting, such research would not be worth the effort.

# 13

## Spiritual Guides

I use the term spiritual guides, or often just guides, but you can call
these entities anything you like. The following is a list of terms that
I have heard other people use:

- Friends (in spirit)
- Totems
- Guardian angels
- Workers
- Helpers
- Upstairs
- The universe
- Ancestors
- One's own higher consciousness

There are many theories about spiritual guides that lay down rules
about the number of guides that a person should have and what it
is that they do, but I don't go along with such rigid rules and
regulations. In time, you will discover who your guides are and
what they do for you. For instance, I know that I have one main
guide, but others come along for particular purposes at certain
times and then disappear again afterwards.

There are two ways of establishing what guides you may have.
One is to use one of the meditations in this book and then ask to be
shown something or someone. Even if nothing happens at the time,
an answer might come along later in a dream or in some other way.

Another method is to visit a medium and ask them to tell you who your guide or guides are. I am not comfortable with this method, as I have been told various things by mediums, but they have rarely connected with anything of which I am aware. There was, however, a psychic artist who once gave me an uncannily accurate illustration of a healing guide whom I happened to have around me at that point.

Most people in the west seem to believe in very exotic guides who come from a very different culture to our own, but I don't know whether this is fact or simply a romantic dramatization of what they want to believe in. Many guides have been involved in some kind of priestly or religious role in their own lifetime, and that does make sense. Some guides have been medical practitioners, leaders in industry or politics, or they may have protected the community in which they had lived. Guides are rarely as mundane as an ex-farm worker, a factory worker or even a village vicar, but there is no reason why they should not be so.

There is also a theory that guides appear in the form that is most likely to appeal to you. If someone tells you that you have a guide or that you have lived in a situation that doesn't ring true, ignore him.

### *Angels*

Before moving on to an exercise for locating your guide, I would like to mention angels. Many people have experiences where they feel that they have been contacted by the kind of angel with which we are familiar from bible stories. In past ages, this kind of vision could have led the person to become a religious Christian, but now people seem to accept that they can come into contact with an angel without necessarily becoming a devout Christian. If an angel contacts you, be very grateful, because it is a rare experience.

Wiccans, pagans, Qabalists and others invoke the help of certain angels to help with their rituals, and this can be a very powerful aid to whatever they are trying to achieve. If you want to learn about this aspect of psychic work, you should look out for good quality books on these subjects. In the Jewish tradition, angels are always male.

### Learning to channel

You can join a spiritualist group and "sit in circle". This involves going along to a training circle on a weekly basis. A medium will run the circle and he or she will take the students through a variety of exercises. He will also show you how to open up, close down and to protect yourself from evil influences. The problem with this is that you will also be expected to swallow the ruling medium's ideas and opinions wholesale. This is fine if the ideas happen to be tried, tested and sensible, but sometimes they are not. Another problem is that, although there is always much talk among spiritual people of leaving one's ego out of things, this community attracts egotists. Some groups are fine, but others may be filled with unfriendly cliques or envious and unpleasant people. Take care. Try a circle if you like, and if you don't like the vibe there, try another.

### Self-training exercises

If you want to channel, sit quietly with your "client" and mentally ask your spiritual guides or the universe to help you link with the person and to receive a message from anyone who wants to send one through. Wait for a while, concentrating on what you can see with your third eye. You may actually wish to close your eyes while doing this, or you may focus on some plain surface.

Something will pop into your mind's eye, much as though you were replaying some scene that you had previously seen in a television program. You may become aware of a person, a face, a name or pet dog or cat. You may see a building, a room, a piece of jewelry, an object of some kind, or may hear a name or become aware of one. You may become aware of a heavy feeling in some part of your own body. You may see, hear, feel or become aware of just about anything. Pass on anything that you receive, however trivial or peculiar it may be.

Ask your client to confirm that this means something to them, but not to go on at length about it. You will need this confirmation before you can progress further, so tell your client not to sit in silence or to "test" you, but to help you by giving you a brief positive or negative answer to anything that you say.

Impressions, sights, sounds, smells or just a very strong feeling may start to flood in. Pass on anything that you get, ask for confirmation and then move on. When you find the images fading or when you start to feel drained and exhausted, you must stop. Don't do any more that day, or at least take a break and try again later. The moment that you start to get something through you will want to do more, but you will find this very tiring at first, so don't overdo it. Once you start getting something, your client will become so fascinated that he will want you to go on for hours, but you must take control of the situation. It is up to you to set the limits.

### Trance and transfiguration

It is possible that you will pass into a kind of hypnotic trance while doing this work, in that the real, solid world around you starts to fade and you become absorbed by the people and places that you visit. Don't worry about this; you will be able to get back again easily enough. It is possible that you will find even stranger things happening, or that your client will observe strange things happening. For instance, you may start to speak in a different voice to your usual one, perhaps even in the voice of the person or the entity that you are linking with. Your face may melt into something else. You may start to look like your client's guide, or some other entity. This kind of event is called transfiguration. It rarely happens, but you should tell your friend to be prepared for anything.

It sometimes happens that the medium gets a definite feeling about something that the client does not accept. If this happens to you, ask your client to look into the matter. Perhaps you are passing on something that has yet to take place, while sometimes a message means little to your client at the time, but falls into place when he does a little research among his relatives.

### *A story about gravel*

I will end this chapter with a story, and this one occurred when I wasn't even thinking about channeling. I had gone to bed and was happily dozing off when I had the distinct impression that my late aunt, Ann, was standing beside the bed. I mentally asked her what she wanted, and she told me to pass a message to her son, Brian. I asked her what she wanted to tell him, and she replied that I should tell him that he would be all right and that it would end in gravel. "Gravel?" I asked. The vision and the voice were fading but I heard her say, "Yes, tell him about gravel."

The next evening I phoned Brian and his wife, Rosalind, answered the phone. I asked her if everything was all right and she said that Brian was very sick and in bed. She told me that he had a kidney stone. I said to pass on my good wishes and then I told her about the visit that I had had from his mother. She breathed a huge sigh of relief and told me that this was very reassuring. Apparently he had been rambling about being able to see his mother sitting on a chair next to his bed, and both Brian and Rosalind were worried in case this meant that he was going to die. She explained to me that when a kidney stone breaks up naturally, it passes out through the bladder as gravel so this is what would probably happen. A few hours later, Rosalind phoned and told me that Brian was now passing gravel in his water and that he would soon recover.

# 14

## Spiritual Healing

Although the spiritualist movement's central purpose is "proof of survival", many churches offer healing. Healers are not confined to the spiritualist movement and many belong to healing organizations, but there are also many terrific healers who are Pagans, witches, psychics, astrologers and Tarot readers. There are also plenty of people who have nothing to do with psychic work, but who just happen to have discovered that they have this gift. There are faith healers in the Christian church and there is a small group of healing Rabbis who belong to a super-religious group in Golders Green in north London. I haven't looked into Hindu, Muslim, Buddhist and other faiths, but I wouldn't be surprised if they didn't have ministers who can heal.

To some extent, healing comes naturally. The mother who comforts a child and rubs or kisses the bruise better is unwittingly giving the child healing. The man who offers a hand or a hug to a friend who is upset or in pain is giving healing. The friend who listens to a pal who is hurting is giving healing - even if this is only over the phone. Most of this healing is unspectacular, but some healers can give out vibes that a sensitive recipient can feel. There are hands-on healers, absent healers, those who heal by talking to people, and a surprisingly large number who specialize in healing animals.

### A few provisos

If you intend to launch yourself into healing and if you intend to treat the public you will need to be registered with an organization. If you work in the European Union, you must be fully qualified and registered with a healing organization such as the Federation of Spiritual Healers. There are similar organizations in many other countries, and the simplest way to find them nowadays is by searching the Internet.

Never treat strangers while you are alone; work in a group where there are plenty of healers and patients of both sexes present, and always do your work in pairs. This is because healers are vulnerable to accusations of sexual assault. The same thing can be leveled at any kind of Reader or consultant, but the nature of healing means that this poses such a wonderful opportunity for a greedy and destructive legal claim. Those who do cross the line into inappropriate sexual behavior should rightly be locked up, but fortunately these disgusting advantage-takers are few and far between.

If you feel drawn to the world of healing, I strongly urge you to take proper training through some recognized organization, but you can try a little healing on your friends and relatives (and even your pets) in the meantime.

### Exercise in healing

If you fancy trying some hands-on healing, ask a friend who could benefit from a bit of healing to sit on a stool or an upright chair. Open your chakras. Bring down white light that also includes flecks of pale blue or turquoise light. Ask for the healing energy to flow out to the patient from the chakras in the palms of your hands and from those in your fingers.

Focus on your friend for a moment and then put your hands close to the part of the body that you feel drawn to. There is no need to touch the person's body, although nothing bad will happen if you do so. One area that you should never touch is the crown of the patient's head; this is because directing energy onto this area can leave the patient with a splitting headache for some hours afterwards. Concentrate on allowing the healing light and energy to enter your body, run down your arms and out through your hands onto and into the patient.

You can focus on the part of the body that you feel drawn to, despite the fact that this may not be the area that is actually troubling your patient. Acupuncture and reflexology use meridian lines, so they often treat an area of the body that is distant from the seat of pain, and healing can work in a similar way.

If you don't feel drawn to any particular body area, you can pass your hands over your friend's body from the head downward, but do this at a distance of about four to six inches from the person's body. As I said before, nothing dreadful will happen if you touch your patient, but it is easier to focus your mind and to move your hands around if you do not. I have to admit that I usually do feel the need to be in actual contact with a patient, so I will often simply hold the person's arms or hands and pass the healing on in that way. I find that it works best when I hold the person's hand and arm rather like the over-friendly grip used by some American politicians. You can close your eyes if you like, as this may help you to focus on gathering, channeling and passing on the healing energies.

After you have finished healing, ask your friend if he felt anything. He may comment that he felt heat, tingling or some other sensation.

Oddly enough, your "patient" may feel worse for a day or two after the healing than he did before, but this is normal. It is just the body's way of reacting and ridding itself of its illness. Alternatively, he may feel sleepy and relaxed.

I have seen healers demonstrating their art in public in a particularly dramatic and exciting way. These healers will throw imaginary "material" sideways off the patient's body and into the surrounding space, or they will flick and toss it on to the ground. This looks clever, amazing and special and it feeds the healer's ego, but it is no way to work. This behavior may actually unnerve the patient, giving him the feeling that his body was filled with something bad. Apart from being totally unnecessary, it can also be harmful to others. If someone walks through the area that the material has been chucked into, it may stick to him like a virus. If you must throw stuff off a patient's aura, keep a bowl of salt at your feet and put the detritus into that.

Once you have finished giving the healing, wash your hands and forearms thoroughly and close your chakras. As soon as you can, take a thorough shower and imagine clear, healing, spiritual water entering your body and flowing through and out of it. This will wash away anything that might have lodged with you.

### Distant healing

Arrange a time with your sick friend and ask him to concentrate on you at that time. Then call down the light as described above and ask for it to be channeled through you and sent on to your friend. If you are aware of a spiritual guide who helps you to accomplish your healing work, you can suggest that your sick friend concentrate on the name of your guide and to call on him for help whenever the need arises, even without you being informed or involved.

### Crystal healing

We all love to buy those attractive crystals that are now so freely available in gift shops and New Age shops all around the world. We know that they are mystic, spiritual and that they have some value, but we don't necessarily know what that value might be. Crystals are formed from the earth itself, and they are a particularly concentrated form of natural mineral or chemical. They can hold healing or other types of energy within them, so they can be used as an aid to spiritual healing. The practitioner lays the appropriate crystal on a chakra, meridian line or even in the shape of the Qabalah on a person's body, before performing the healing. I have to be honest and tell you that this is not an area of spiritual healing with which I am familiar, and it is definitely a job for an expert, so

I suggest that if you are interested in discovering more about this subject, look for books, courses and information on the Internet.

If you like having crystals around the house, or if you use them in conjunction with Feng Shui or any other system, I suggest that you use any type of spiritual or Wiccan method of stone cleansing. For example, you can wash them in a natural source of water, leave them in the sun to dry and polish them with a new cotton tea cloth before using them.

In Feng Shui, crystals belong to the element of earth, because that is where they come from. If you have a room that is full of colors and objects that belong to the wood, metal, fire and water elements, a few crystals will balance this with some earth energy. Oddly enough, the Chinese associate the earth element with health, so a few calming pink or white quartz crystals or yellow stones may be useful, and they certainly can't do any harm. I read somewhere that computers can be balanced by placing pink quartz and amethyst stones on them, and I have found that this does work. Psychic work (even writing about psychic work) can upset the energies in a computer, so I advise my writers and friends to use these stones on their machines in order to calm them down and balance their energies. Does this sound crazy? Perhaps, but it works, so I suggest that you just take this one on trust - after all, it can't do any harm to you or your computer.

# 15

## Scrying and Gazing

Scrying is an old-fashioned word for seeing into something. If you read historical novels, you may read that someone has descried a person in the distance, and this means that they have discovered the person by looking for or at them. The method that everyone understands is crystal gazing, but some seers prefer to use a convex dish that has a shiny black glazed finish, called a scrying dish. A scryer can use a candle flame, the flames in a fire or even clouds in the sky. Cloud scrying is common in southern Africa.

The two friends who helped me with the information in this chapter both work in different ways. They talk about crystal gazing, but the same information can be applied to a scrying dish. I can't think of anything more to tell you than to try their methods for yourself and see whether they work for you.

### Robin Lown

Robin is a palmist, Tarot Reader, clairvoyant and crystal Reader, and he is on the committee of the British Astrological and Psychic Society. This side of his life exists in addition to him having a "proper job" as an inspector of schools within the British education system. This is what Robin had to tell me about crystal gazing.

### Setting the scene

If you want to buy a crystal ball, visit a psychic festival or a shop specializing in these things and have a good look at what is available. Weigh the crystals that you like in your hand and see which ones you feel drawn to, because the shape and size is important. You may even fancy a colored crystal for your readings. Never buy any item of this nature by mail order, because you need to try it to see if it feels right. Having said this, most professionals seem to have had their crystals given to them or bought for them, or they seem to acquire their crystal in some odd way.

Before trying to use your crystal, wash it thoroughly in spring water and leave it out in the sun to dry. Then, meditate on it, asking for it to work for you and also to bring help and guidance to those who consult you. I charged my own crystal by holding it in my hands within my aura and telling the spirit world that I wanted to use it in order to give help, service and truth to those who needed it. I meditated on it as being part of myself, re-affirming myself as a seeker of truth. Even now when using my crystal, my motives have to be clear. I must want to be of service and help to the Enquirer, because any other feelings would disrupt the reading, and I would have to start over again. Most people respect the crystal for what it is and ask permission before picking it up. I have noticed that only crass materialists and those who are totally unaware of spiritual matters attempt to pick it up without asking permission, and I am afraid that I get quite shirty with them when this happens.

### *How do I read?*

I use palmistry first, in order to create a link with the Enquirer, and then I give them the crystal to hold. I tell them that it is not necessary for them to think of anything in particular. After this, I ask for the crystal back and I place it on a stand, which is on a piece of black cloth. Then I slowly tune in. I use the crystal as a form of psychometry and I don't think that I actually see anything in the crystal itself. Rather, I see images that are projected from my head in a kind of psychic ventriloquism and a projection of what is in my mind.

Firstly, I see scenes, people and situations, and then I begin to feel impressions and emotions. My method is definitely allied to psychometry, clairvoyance, clairaudience and clairsentience.

I asked Robin whether crystal reading had ever led him to mediumistic experiences where he was in contact with friends or relatives of the Enquirer who had "passed over". He said that this did happen on occasion and that there were also times when he felt himself being "taken over" by someone who wanted to express his or her thoughts through him.

At this point, I obviously don't know whether the images that I see are of the past, present or future, so I inwardly ask my Guiding Spirit to tell me. I ask whether this is the past and then wait until I get a yes or no feeling. If the event turns out to be in the past, I ask to be shown what relevance this might have to the present - and this often brings another image to me.

By now, I will be aware that my Chakras are open and that both the crystal and the Enquirer are within my auric bubble. (The Chakras are the seven psychic centers in the body that have to open up in order to allow psychic impressions to flow in and out). I then start to tell the Enquirer what I am receiving. As he or she begins to connect with what I am saying, the images and impressions speed up and become more definite, more certain - and then it becomes much easier for me.

Sometimes an Enquirer can block me, either because he is skeptical or for some other reason. Then I see or feel only a shaft of light, as though it were coming down a tunnel, at which point I give up and resort to reading the Enquirer's palm or cards, both of which are less subject to psychic disturbance.

I then asked Robin how long he would spend on a reading like this, and he said that it depended upon the rapport that he had with the Enquirer and the amount of information that came through. He told me that he always finished a reading by giving a summary of the main points as he saw them. He also kept a pencil and a pad of paper nearby so that he could sketch an item if he wanted to (Robin is artistic). He also told me that he tended to see certain particular symbols while his centers were opening up. One of them was the figure of eight symbol for infinity that appears over the Magician's head in the Tarot deck, the other was the caduceus, which is the winged staff carried by the Roman god, Mercury, which signifies enlightenment, healing abilities and magical powers.

### Barbara Ellen

Barbara is a full-time professional clairvoyant and medium. She is also a consultant for the British Astrological and Psychic Society. Barbara has had many years of experience; she is highly trained, very skilled and knowledgeable. Although Barbara is not primarily a crystal gazer (she tells me that she finds pure clairvoyance quicker and easier), she can use a crystal ball very well when she is required to do so. This is what Barbara told me.

### Preparing a new crystal ball

It is far better to acquire a crystal than to buy a new one; wherever your crystal has come from, the first thing you need to do is to immerse it for twelve hours in salted spring water. Some Readers use a solution of vinegar and water. After this, wash the crystal under running water, ideally from some natural source, such as a waterfall or a stream. If you haven't access to a stream, find something that will collect fresh rainwater and then allow the water to flow over the ball. Polish the crystal with a chamois leather and leave it in the sunlight for at least four hours. After that, don't allow anyone else to touch or even to look into your crystal.

### Training and preparation

Some Readers spin the crystal with a finger while they are tuning themselves in, while many others work from mental impressions (as Robin does), but I try to use the crystal itself.

Place the crystal on a small plinth that is covered by a black cloth. Ideally the cloth should be silk, because this is a completely natural product, although many Readers prefer to use velvet because it has a denser texture. Partially cover or surround the crystal with a second black cloth, which should definitely be made of silk. If you wish, you can darken the room slightly and put on a dim light. Some Readers use a red light, as this is known to draw the spirit world close.

Practice sessions should always be carried out at the same time of the day and never late at night - this procedure seems to help our spiritual guides to work better. Cup the crystal in the cloth and bring it up so that it is in front of your forehead - that is, close to, but not touching the "third eye", which is in the center of your forehead. While training, you must keep the crystal within your aura. This means keeping it wrapped in its silk or velvet cloths on a table next to you while you sleep, read, and watch television, etc., or in a bag at your side while out and about. Never try to read on a full stomach or if you are upset or angry.

Do some yoga breathing each time before you start training or reading. To do this, breath in from the stomach for a count of four, hold your breath for a count of two and let it out on a count of four. Do this exercise four times. Relax, get yourself into a peaceful state of mind and then go ahead.

If you begin to see symbols in the crystal during this time, note them down. You may be aware of certain symbols that are personal to you, such as a black cat, a white rabbit and so on. Keep a note of what these mean and build up a vocabulary of signs and symbols.

The crystal should begin to cloud, and it is important that when this happens that you remain calm and not let yourself become over-excited, or the vision will disappear. Red or orange "smoke" is a warning of danger, blue or green "smoke" is fine. Objects that are colored red or orange are a different thing altogether, because only red "smoke" is a warning to be on the alert.

The visions will go out of focus and then come back sharply into focus, but you will have to wait a few minutes for this to happen - perhaps as long as five minutes. This training period will last for about eight days, but you must persevere with it until the ability comes. When an image comes, wait for the message that comes with it. This message will come into your mind through the help of your Spiritual Guides.

Sometimes the objects will come into view first and the clouds later, because every Reader works slightly differently. Be sure to ask your Spiritual Guides to help you.

When I see images moving in the crystal, I know that those that come in from the left represent events that are coming towards the Enquirer while those on or travelling towards the right are passing away from him. This is how it works for me, but you may see things or do things differently.

As soon as you feel that you are making a link with your crystal, either with mental pictures or actually seeing milky-type smoke or images within the ball itself, find some guinea pigs to sit for you. Try to find people about whom you know nothing. Ask your Enquirer to cup his or her hands around the crystal without actually touching it, and to remain in that position for approximately two minutes. Then take the crystal back from the Enquirer and relax. Shade the crystal from the light and begin to give out whatever comes to you. As soon as the Enquirer can acknowledge that you are getting something meaningful through, further images will come through even more quickly. Any kind of feedback will help. Be sure to keep notes so that you can assess your progress and make adjustments in your thinking.

### *A sample reading*

At this point, Barbara went on to give me a reading. I hadn't expected this, so it was an unaccustomed treat. The first thing that she saw was an airplane. This was not surprising, as I traveled a lot at that time and I was due to take a trip to New York in the near future. She then saw my son Stuart waving a document of some kind. Stuart was about to take an exam in computer and business studies. Barbara also told me that she could see my husband with a pain in his back and leg. This was not surprising as my then husband, Tony Fenton, had been doing some heavy work and his back was never strong at the best of times. She then told me that my daughter, Helen, needed new glasses. As it happened, Helen had recently had some new spectacles, so that didn't make much sense at the time. However, it turned out a few days later that the prescription was wrong and the shop had to make up replacement lenses for her, so this was a good example of the way that some readings may not make sense until some time later.

# 16

## Near Death Experiences

***Yesterday was a very interesting day...***

I have spent the past couple of weeks tidying up the final draft of this book, and it has not turned out to be an easy thing to do. The book itself is no problem, but Jan and I are going through one of those phases when one thing after another has gone wrong, so the book is taking much longer than it should do. Simple journeys have turned into nightmares, and we have had to make a number of long train and road journeys recently, physically draining both of us. Two of our computers, which are essential for our work, suddenly broke down within a week of each other, and a series of plumbing problems have meant that the plumber has spent so much time in our house that he has practically started paying rent.

On Sunday, Jan's elderly mother was rushed into hospital. Normally I look after her needs, but the day after she was taken ill, I went down with a high fever and a very sore throat, which turned out to be a form of influenza. A day after this, a tooth that the dentist and I have been nursing along for the past couple of years suddenly went into overdrive.

The following day, I was lucky enough to get an emergency appointment with the dentist. She looked at the tooth, declared it a hopeless case and promptly extracted it. The extraction didn't go well. The crown of the tooth snapped and it seemed that the three roots were all over the place, so the dentist had to cut them into bits and take them out piece by piece. The physical shock to my system, at a time when I was already ill and thoroughly exhausted by nights without sleep during the preceding weeks, suddenly caught up with me.

I felt my body becoming extremely light and I became aware that I was rising up from the operating chair. The discomfort of the extraction no longer bothered me, as it was now all happening to the very solid body that was still lying in the dentist chair below me. I felt myself reach a position where I was suspended about two inches above the redundant body below. Instinctively, I looked up to the left, towards the corner of the room and I saw the glowing pewter colored entrance to a tunnel. The entrance was not large, but it was large enough for me to get into. I didn't feel especially happy, sad, frightened or glad - I would say that my greatest feeling was that of curiosity. Then I heard my late mother's voice from far off shouting at me and telling me to go back as "it wasn't time yet". I also saw my long dead father looking over her shoulder, and he had a very concerned look on his face. I mentally asked them if I had long to go on this earth and they assured me that I had. The next thing I knew was that I was back in my body and the dentist was tugging at the last piece of root, which was still resisting her efforts to get it out.

## *Near death experiences*

Near death experiences are so well documented as to be a mainstream belief rather than a notion confined to those who take up spiritual or psychic work. Those who have these experiences usually report that they left their bodies, floated upwards and then hovered in a corner of the ceiling. Most say that they could see their physical bodies lying beneath them. (I didn't get high enough to see myself lying there yesterday, but I was aware of the physical body beneath me).

Many people report seeing a bright light that they felt drawn to, and that they started to move towards this light. Others talk of a journey through a tunnel or over a dark body of water before encountering this light. All those who "come back," say that they felt an immeasurable sense of peace and happiness as they approached the "other side". They also say that they felt as though they wanted or perhaps even longed to move towards the light. Some report that after taking the journey, they stood at the entrance to a beautiful garden. Many tell of meeting relatives who have gone before them, telling them that they should go back because it is not yet time for them to pass over. Some are happy to be sent back, while others are less so, but all say that they will never fear death after this experience.

Medical people suggest that it is the lack of oxygen within the brain of the sick person, or perhaps the drugs that he has been given that induce euphoric dreams of this kind. This may have made sense to me until yesterday, but now it doesn't. The experience is a spiritual one rather than a medical one. It is often possible to produce plausible alternative explanations for various mystifying events, but that does not automatically mean that cynics are correct in their assumptions, especially where psychic phenomena are concerned.

By the same token, one does not have to accept things blindly. For instance, my husband, Jan, has never had a near death experience, despite having been knocked unconscious a couple of times and having been under general anesthetic a number of times. For him, near death experience is just a relatively meaningless label (and hopefully will stay just that!). Jan has lived with me long enough to be well aware that it would be impossible for me to fool him and everyone else, regularly and consistently, regarding my psychic abilities. His view is that one must have an open mind, and to accept that sometimes, things do exist that not everyone is capable of experiencing directly.

I have heard accounts of psychics who have been with someone as they died, and they report seeing the person's ethereal body leave the physical body and move upwards. The two bodies appear to be attached by a silvery "umbilical" cord, which becomes thinner as it unwinds, and then breaks to allow the ethereal body to move up and away.

### *Autosuggestion or the real thing?*

Skeptics are quick to say that near death experience is so well documented that we expect to have this experience if we are seriously ill. They quote that the experience is shown on films and television, so we are all aware of it. This is simply not true in all cases.

My first husband, Tony Fenton, was rushed into hospital with appendicitis at the age of four. This being 1935, he had never seen a film, and television had not yet been invented, so he couldn't have been influenced by anything. He went through the whole experience, right up to meeting his grandparents at the gate of a lovely garden. They told him to go back as it wasn't time for him to join them. Many years later, when the time eventually came that Tony really was dying, he was sad about it but he was not afraid. A week before Tony died, I was walking upstairs in the house when I saw his long dead mother floating down the stairs. She came towards me and then passed me - apparently without noticing my presence. At this point, I knew for sure that he was on his way over.

My mother was at home when she fell ill for the last time. I had visited her over the previous couple of weeks, while she was still very alert, but I was aware that she was nearing the end of her days here. When she was clearly dying, my daughter and I went to see her, but when we arrived at her home, we found that she was already in a coma. My distraught stepfather was standing at the foot of the bed, but while he was talking to us, Helen and I became aware of another presence standing beside him. My step-dad told us that the last thing my mother had done before sinking into the coma, was to sit up and ask him in a rather impatient tone of voice why he wasn't dressed and ready to go out.

The pair of them had been keen ballroom dancers, and my mother had danced right up to about six weeks before she died. Apparently, when she had asked Sam this question, he had laughingly replied that he wasn't going anywhere. When Sam told Helen and me this tale, we both looked at each other, but said nothing. We could see that mother was definitely on her way to a dance - but not with Sam! The vision that we saw at the end of her bed was of my very handsome and long-dead father, and he had also been her dancing partner in earlier years. Thus, my mother literally danced off the face of this earth!

I adored my father, but he died at the age of thirty-eight from a heart condition. A couple of days after his death, I dreamed that I was following him down a long tunnel. This was something like a subway tunnel, apart from the fact that there was no railway and that the arched roof and the floor seemed to glow like well-polished pewter. I ran as hard as I could to catch up my father and I called out to him repeatedly, but he didn't appear to be able to hear me. He kept up a steady walking pace, but moved faster away from me. It was as though he was walking along one of those moving walkways that we see in airports. I began to see a thin new-moon shaped glow of intense light in the distance, rather as though a door at the end of the tunnel was slightly ajar. I wanted to reach my father before he disappeared into this light, but something prevented me, so I turned back disconsolately and retraced my steps. I adored my father and I am happy to know that, when my time comes, that I will be able to see him again.

Obviously, there are no exercises that you can do in connection with this part of the spiritual experience, but I guess it is comforting to know that dying is not nearly as difficult as living may be.

# 17

## Past Lives

During one of my school years, our class had an excellent geography teacher who taught us a great deal about India and also about Hindu and Buddhist beliefs. This woman was an early immigrant to Britain from the sub-continent, so she was able to tell us about the country and its people with far more authority than a teacher who had gathered information from dry textbooks. She told us that Buddhists and others in India were often vegetarians (vegetarianism was unusual in Britain in those days). They sincerely believed that any one of us might have been an animal in a previous life and that we may become one again in a subsequent life, so flesh eating was tantamount to cannibalism.

Once I got into psychic work, I discovered that many people believed in past lives, although not perhaps to the point of believing that we transmuted to and from the animal kingdom. The theory is that we have lived many times before and that we will live many times in the future, until we learn enough to move into the realms of the heavens. Apparently, even ancient Jewish and Christian texts showed a belief in reincarnation in the distant past, but it is said that politically correct scribes later wrote these out of the bible and other texts. I have subsequently had enough evidence myself to firmly believe in reincarnation.

## *Déjà vu*

The words "déjà vu" mean already seen. This strange phenomenon occurs when a person visits a place that he has never seen before, but he feels that he knows it well. Some people can lead others around such an area, pointing out things before they reach them, as though they were revisiting a place where they once lived. Sometimes the area is not quite as they expect it to be, although when they investigate old records, they discover that their "memories" are of the place as it once was.

## *A tale of two Australians*

Several years ago, British television ran a fascinating television program about two Australian women who had felt strongly drawn to places in Britain. The program makers took the first woman to a village in England, and to a farm where she said she had worked as a young woman in a previous life. With the absolute certainty of someone who knew where she was going, she took them to an old barn where she said that she had milked cows and goats.

She looked down at the beaten earth floor and commented sadly that she was disappointed, because in her "memory" the floor had been covered in flagstones, and furthermore that there had been an unusual design on one in the middle of the floor. The woman even made a diagram of the design. The present farmer was adamant that the barn floor had never ever been different. The program makers asked the farmer if they could borrow a shovel and dig down, provided that they put the floor back the way it was after they had finished. They didn't have to dig far, because they soon struck stone. Sure enough, a few inches beneath the earth floor, there was a wonderful old stone-slab floor, and the central slab had the design engraved in it that the woman had drawn for them.

The second woman swore that she had been a surgeon in a hospital in Edinburgh in a previous life. She described the rooms in which she had studied and worked, and she even drew detailed plans of the layout of the building. The program makers took her to an old hospital in Edinburgh that seemed to fit the bill, but the layout of the place was wrong. However, an old caretaker told them that the hospital had not always been the way it is now, and that they should search for the plans to the original layout. When they did this, the plans turned out to be identical to those that the woman had drawn.

One person I know really fancies herself, and she is convinced that she was Mary, Queen of Scots in a previous life. Well, she does have red hair and bad taste in men, so perhaps she is right! There are many people who are convinced that they were Cleopatra in a previous life. Who's to say that a clever girl like Cleo can only reincarnate into one body at a time?

My present husband, Jan, thinks that there may be a logical (that's Jan) explanation for the problem of how so many people can all claim to have been the same, usually famous person, in a past life: Jan's view is as follows... firstly, perhaps all of time exists all the time, as is becoming evident even in scientific circles nowadays. Secondly, in that case, perhaps all the people throughout history, past, present and future exist, and are used, in the way we use our films; instead of us saying "I'm off to see the latest Harry Potter movie", perhaps our spirits decide "I think I'll go down and be Julius Caesar this time". As Jan says, it's a far bigger step to accept the concept of past lives at all than it is to accept the idea of such "life movies". I can't argue with that typically Aquarian viewpoint, and until such time that one concept or the other is categorically proved correct, I believe it is up to each of us to use with whatever viewpoint works best for us, as long as it doesn't harm anyone else.

Several years ago, Jan and I decided to take a weekend break in the beautiful city of Bath in southwest England. We couldn't find accommodation in Bath, so we ended up in the nearby city of Bristol. I have visited Bristol several times, but this was Jan's first visit there. I find the layout of Bristol confusing and I often get lost while driving or walking round the city. As soon as we neared the older part of the city, Jan seemed to know his way around and drove about quite happily. That evening, Jan took me walking around the quaint streets, complete with ancient pubs and interesting shops in rickety old buildings, as though he knew the place well. Jan has no family connections with Britain at all, so there was no possible family history or connection involved.

### *Lodges*

Another form of déjà vu happens when you meet someone with whom you feel extraordinarily comfortable and it feels as though you are related to the person. This feeling transcends the fact that you may be different ages or from a completely different culture, class, race, financial bracket, and educational background. This is a kind of immediate recognition between souls. Oddly enough, such a meeting doesn't mean that you will automatically spend that much time together in this life, but it is likely you will do something good for each other, then perhaps move on and lose touch with each other again.

There are two theories here. The first is that you knew each other (and presumably liked one another) in a previous life. The second is that you belong to the same lodge on the other side. This implies that you belonged to the same group in the spirit world before you were born and that you will see each other again later. My friend, Jonathan Dee, has a theory based on the Qabalah that fits this, as different people are linked to different Sephirot (segments) of the Qabalah.

### *Unreasonable dislike*

Psychologists tell us that there are logical reasons for us to take an inexplicable, spontaneous dislike to someone, or for someone else to loathe us on sight. For instance, there may be something about us that reminds them of someone they have had problems with in the past, or they may have preconceived notions about certain types of people. All this is true enough, but there may also be a previous life connection. I can't be definite about this, but it seems logical that just as we can click with certain people who share our lodge, so can we dislike others for a similar spiritual reason.

## *Phobias*

Some people have strange phobias that cannot be explained away. I am not talking about those who are neurotic or mentally ill, but about ordinary people who just can't bear something or who feel afraid of something for no good reason. Such phobias may be related to a previous life experience.

## *Discover your previous life*

If you wish to look into the possibility of finding out if you have had lived before; you will need to enlist the aid of a decent qualified and registered hypnotist. You will also need a tape recorder. Ask the hypnotist to regress you back beyond this life, and not to wipe your mind of your experiences once you return from your journey. As long as the session is recorded, you won't lose anything that you cannot quite remember.

There are also psychics who specialize in past life regression, and it may be worth making inquiries in your area, if the thought of regression appeals to you.

For that matter, you may also be able to track down psychics who do "progressions", or future life inquiries. This is a novel concept which I have had little time or opportunity to pursue, but you may wish to do some research into this interesting subject yourself, helped by the wonderful resource we know as the Internet - how on earth did we manage before it evolved?

# 18

## Holding a Séance

We all know what should happen when we hold a séance, because we have seen them portrayed in films and on the television. The general idea is that a group of people sits in circle holding hands and then they ask the spirits to pay them a visit. Naturally, films and television dramatize this, to the point where tables rattle and things fly round the room, but most real séances aren't this interesting.... or are they?

### *Exercise in holding your own séance*
Gather a group of friends around and make them comfortable. If you wish, you can offer them a drink and a cookie or two. British readers will automatically offer tea, instant coffee and biscuits or small cakes. A small glass of beer, wine or sherry won't hurt, because this will relax everyone, but more than a small amount of alcohol, or a heavy meal before conducting the séance, will block everyone's chakras. Give your pals a meal and drinks after the event by all means, if you wish.

The only piece of equipment that you will need is a red light bulb that you can fit into table lamp, or you can use a red lampshade over an ordinary light. You can also use one of those fiber-optic lamps and fix it so that it is stuck on red. The red light is intended to enable the spirits to come through easily. Gather your friends and sit them around a table or on chairs arranged in a circle. Designate one person to lead the séance. Once the group has settled down and is sitting quietly, the leader should open his chakras and then say a prayer in order to protect the group. The following prayer should do the job:

> *I call upon my spiritual guides (giving their names if known),*
> *And guides of all who are present,*
> *To protect us from harmful or evil spirits,*
> *And allow us to learn and experience whatever is sent to us,*
> *From the spiritual realms, in peace, love and harmony.*

The leader can choose to end the prayer with the Wiccan words of, "So mote it be" or "Amen" or the old English for amen, which is, "So be it".

The leader should take the group through the chakra opening meditation and perhaps another relaxing meditation as well, but doing the chakra opening one, as a group, will be fine. The group should now all hold hands, as this creates a link between each person and increases the power of the group as a whole. The leader should then ask the spirits to come near and the group should sit quietly and wait for something to happen.

One person might start to feel a "presence" and the room may suddenly feel cold, or there may even be some kind of glow or strange light. One person may fall into a slight trance and start to pass on feelings and messages that they receive. This person may still sound like themselves, albeit a bit dazed and sleepy - or their voice may change, depending upon whom they are channeling through.

Another possibility is that one of the group will turn out to be a "rescue" medium. This usually only happens when the medium is skilled, but it can happen to an untrained one. The medium will start to describe a scene where he can "see" someone who has died suddenly and who doesn't realize what has happened. The group will then ask the dead person to look upwards, to see a light somewhere above him and then tell him to go to the light. When the medium sees the spirit moving up and into the light and then disappearing from sight, the group will know that the person has been "rescued".

Sometimes a spirit finds it hard to get through to the group, so he may cause "disturbances" such as tapping, moving things around or making the lights flash. The only thing is to keep the chakras well open and to concentrate on trying to communicate with the frustrated spirit.

### Ouija boards

Most people have heard of Ouija boards. The word is usually pronounced wee-gee or wee-jar, though it is actually composed of the French and German words for "yes", which are "oui" and "ja". Frankly I don't recommend using the Ouija method, as it seems to encourage particularly nasty spirits, although I don't know why this should be so. Perhaps this is because untrained people often experiment with Ouija and they don't know how to ask for helpful spirits or for protection.

It is possible to buy commercially produced Ouija boards, but most people write all the letters of the alphabet on pieces of paper and then add two more pieces of paper with the words "yes" and "no" on them. The letters of the alphabet are arranged in an oval on a table with the "yes and no" pieces at either end. The only other piece of equipment needed is a wine glass. Several people each place a finger on the wine glass, and the designated leader asks the famous question, "Is anyone there?" The glass then gradually moves to the "yes" position. Frankly, it is never likely to go to the "no" position, as some joker will be bound to start the session by pushing it around for a laugh. Then the leader asks who is present or what message they wish to convey. The glass then slowly moves from one letter to the next and so on until it has spelled out a sentence.

### The drunken revel

Those who are most likely to try the Ouija are young people who have had a fair bit to drink. I am the first to admit that I did my share of this in my youth, although I was never a big drinker because I don't have a good head for it. Alcohol switches off the normal, logical, day-to-day thinking processes and allows a person to relax and lose his inhibitions. It is definitely not a good party game - for a start, it is too easy for someone to manipulate the movement of the glass. Somehow, the combination of youthful ignorance, lots of booze and the Ouija can lead to some pretty horrendous experiences. I tried it once again later, under strictly controlled circumstances, but when messages came through, they were still not pleasant.

It appears that the Ouija really does focus on unhappiness, shock and disasters, which is why there are messages about mugging, stabbing, serious illness and death. I once witnessed the fury of someone who had passed over and whose will had not been carried out in the way that they had wanted. In short, the Ouija works - but the results are so unpleasant and the feeling that it leaves behind is so depressing that it isn't worth doing. I don't think I would use it for a client even if I were asked to.

# 19

## Who You Gonna Call? Ghostbusters!

Not everyone believes in ghosts, but they are real enough. People who have no awareness will tell you that that they don't believe in ghosts, but if they were to spend their whole lives indoors with the curtains closed, they probably wouldn't believe that there was a world outside their house either. You don't have to believe friends who tell fanciful ghost stories, but you do need to keep an open mind.

Sometimes a person who has never had any dealings with spiritual matters can be taken by surprise. I remember one perfectly ordinary neighbor of ours who started "hearing things" and feeling a presence after his beloved wife died. It was their close relationship during their time on earth and his grief that had opened him to the spirit world and to the fact that his wife was trying to contact him.

There are many theories about ghosts, and I am afraid that I don't have any definitive answers, but it seems that some souls don't make the journey to "the other side" after they have died. In some cases, a person dies under unpleasant circumstances and this keeps them attached to their last known address. Some have only recently died and have not yet made the trip across. Some are tied by grief to a person who they have left on earth, though it seems more likely that it is the earth-bound person's grief that keeps the spirit from making his journey. Sometimes the ghost has passed over but feels the need to pop back from time to time. The following amusing tale is about a spirit who probably regretted the lack of a physical body.

### The blue light

When I was in my teens, I worked on the stage as a dancer, singer, acrobat, and actor. On one occasion, I was working in a show in the north of England, and as I had little money to spare, I shared a room in the digs with a very nice singer called Pearl. The room was large and it contained a huge double bed that I slept in, and a single bed in a corner that Pearl opted for.

After the first night, Pearl confessed that she felt uneasy in her bed, and on the following night when she got into bed, she felt even uneasier. Despite the fact that it was a warm summer, Pearl had also commented that she had felt very cold in that bed. When she climbed into bed on the second night, I looked over to her corner and to my amazement, I saw a blue glow hovering over her bed. That was more than enough for Pearl! She scampered over to my bed and we spent the remainder of our time sharing the large double. It may be worth noting that it was not unusual for two women to share a bed in those days, and nobody thought anything of it.

Towards the end of our stay, I packed our gear while Pearl popped downstairs to see our landlady and to pay our rent. When she returned to our room to collect her suitcase, she looked pale and concerned. When I asked her what had happened, she told me that she had seen the landlady handing some black clothing to a neighbor. The landlady had then turned to Pearl and commented that her husband had recently passed away, and that he had done so in the single bed in our room!

Once Pearl had recovered from the shock we had a good laugh about it. The poor man must have been amazed to find two attractive young women in his room - and moreover, one of them sleeping in his bed! At long last, his dearest wish had come true, but he was not in a position to take advantage of it!

### *Animal rights*

I once lived in a house that was haunted by a tabby cat. I saw it in various rooms, but mainly in my son, Stuart's bedroom. Apparently the previous occupants of the house also had a son and this lad had been a radio-ham who had spent many happy hours tuning into Timbuktu and whatnot in that room. The cat had apparently snoozed happily on the floor close by him while he twiddled his switches.

Despite the fact that the cat had long gone from this earth, it must have been pleased to have a nice lad back in the room - and it obviously didn't mind Stuart's teenage mess! Also, Stuart likes animals, so he was happy to allow the cat's spirit to stay. Visiting psychics would sometimes comment on my nice cat - usually without even realizing that it was a very low-maintenance variety in terms of cat food and vet's bills.

### *What should you do if you encounter a ghost?*

The answer to this depends upon a number of variables. If you feel a sense that someone is near you, and as long as you are comfortable with it, just leave it alone. It may be that a loved-one has popped back for a while to keep an eye on you. If you visit a place that feels haunted, allow yourself to relax into a slight trance state and then mentally ask the spirit who he is and what he wants. If you are made to feel at all uncomfortable by any kind of ghostly presence, call in a decent professional psychic to find out what the ghost wants and to move him to the other side.

### *Exercise for seeing ghosts*

By now you probably have a fair idea of how to do this. Open your chakras, sit quietly and mentally ask if there is anyone there. If you get a feeling about something or somebody, ask them who they are and if they are happy. If they appear keen to communicate, let them. After this, tell them that they can go to the light if they want to, but that they are welcome to pop back from time to time if they feel like it. Ask them to ensure that they do no damage on any subsequent visits and that they avoid frightening those who live in the house.

### Another ghost story

I simply can't leave this subject without telling you my favorite ghost story.

Many years ago, my mother lived in an apartment where there was a very nice young couple living next door. I shall call these neighbors Andrea and Jim. Andrea and Jim had three lovely children and they were happy until Jim fell ill. Sadly, it turned out that Jim had inoperable stomach cancer. During the course of Jim's illness, Andrea had turned for comfort to another neighbor, who I will call Tom, and this relationship had become an affair. Before you become too judgmental about this situation, it is not uncommon for anyone to turn to another for support and affection when in such dire straits. The partner who is doing the caring can feel overwhelmed by sadness and helplessness, while a sick or dying partner can make life stressful by becoming understandably self-absorbed, irritable and depressed. In the event, there must have been more to this arrangement than just comfort and sex, because almost immediately after Jim died, Tom left his own wife and moved in with Andrea and her three children.

A couple of weeks later, Andrea told my mother that she and Tom were moving away. When my mother asked why this was, Andrea told her that every time she and Tom had tried to make love, the bedclothes would be snatched off them. Worse still, on one occasion, Jim's slippers that were still lying in the corner of the bedroom had started to "walk" across the room. It doesn't take a super-brain to work out that Jim was not happy with the Tom and Andrea situation, or the fact that this was going on in his bedroom!

### Poltergeists

This German word means "noisy spirit", referring to the ones that throw things around and frighten people; naturally, makers of horror-films just love to portray them. Poltergeist activity can range from mild tapping, lights turning on and off and doors being slammed, to things flying around and even to a place being thoroughly trashed. Mild disturbances such as tapping are mainly due to the kind of ghostly events that I described earlier, where a person in spirit is trying to communicate without success, but true poltergeist activity is really awful.

There seem to be a number of possible sources for poltergeist activity. The first is that an entity (and perhaps one that is not pleasant) is desperate to gain attention, but other such apparitions seem to emanate from those who are actually suffering from the activity. In this case, it is the kinetic energy within the disturbed person, or the disturbed atmosphere within the location, that is the cause.

Poltergeist activity often seems to occur around adolescent children. It may be related to the way that their hormones and brains are changing at that time, but it often occurs in a household where there is great unhappiness and a very uncomfortable atmosphere.

It seems that we all contain kinetic energy that can be released. When someone throws a ball, he draws his arm back, then thrusts it forward and releases the ball; the kinetic energy is then transferred to the ball so that it flies through the air. The same kind of thing is apparent in a light airplane when the pilot revs the engine and then releases the brakes. This can be set off by adults, children of any age or it can sometimes be set off by adults who are severely sexually frustrated, but it does seem to affect children who are approaching adolescence more than any other group.

I remember hearing about a household in which a mother of such a family of children was being attacked by flying objects, to the point where these things were bruising and cutting her. The family called in a psychic exorcist and that helped, but the real improvement came when the warring parents parted and both moved out of the house and into separate dwellings.

If the poltergeist activity stems from a spirit trying to catch someone's attention, then it is best to call in an exorcist medium to find out what's on its mind. He will then lead it gently to the light and over to the other side.

### *Elementals*

If there is one thing I am known for, it is the ability to explain difficult ideas and concepts in a way that makes them easier to grasp and understand. Now, when it comes to elementals, my talent is being stretched to the limit, because I am going to tell about something that doesn't exist - until something happens to make it exist, that is....

There are four elements on earth, these being fire, earth, air and water. All four are necessary to life on our planet, but when any one of them gets out of control, they become destructive. A wind can clear the air and dry the washing, but too much wind is destructive. In addition, a fire can warm a house or burn it to the ground, while water can be used to bathe in or to drown someone in. However, there is a fifth element and this one is etheric or spiritual, and like the other four elements, it can take forms that are either beneficial or frightening.

We all know what it feels like to visit a happy house and we also know what an unhappy and uncomfortable atmosphere feels like. Misery or anger can permeate the very stones of a building, to the extent that once the people who lived there have moved on, the atmosphere can remain unchanged. Some cities have an edgy atmosphere that is made up of furious business trading and smart shops that lie alongside dirty, unkempt streets filled with drunks, druggies and a heavy atmosphere of danger. The ambition, drive, greed and high energy permeate the place, and seemingly attract a counter energy of dirt, misery, self-destruction and danger.

Elementals are not the spirits of dead people, but something that is created out of the ether by the emotions of people, and even perhaps animals and plants that inhabit a place. These elementals will form in a shape that means something to those who encounter them - either as a pleasant form or as a very nasty one. The surrounding atmosphere then turns this energy into something that can be seen with the inner eye and sometimes also with our two ordinary eyes as well.

The entity that is created can be pleasant, inspirational, protective, uplifting and inspiring, and this is the source of such beings as fairies, leprechauns, elves and other such entities that people really do occasionally see. It is likely that those who see such things do so as much with their third or inner eye as with their physical eyes, but they certainly do see them. The same goes for angels, religious visions and so on. The same kind of energy can form into a religious vision, such as the Virgins of Fatima or Lourdes or the visions that Joan of Arc witnessed.

There are Tibetan adepts who "create" these beings out of the atmosphere, so that they can be felt by other sensitive people. Whether deliberately or accidentally created, the vision would look different when seen by a Tibetan, a Native American, an Australian Aborigine or an African, whose power, need or deep belief brings the elemental to life.

Unpleasant elementals also exist. The vast majority of these are created by accident, but some are deliberately created. The theory goes that an elemental that is deliberately created is not a happy bunny, and that it eventually turns upon its creator. We all know the fable of Doctor Frankenstein, who created a monster who ultimately, turned upon him. Another version is that of Doctor Jekyll and his alter ego, Mr. Hyde, who eventually destroyed his master and himself.

The late Dion Fortune tells a story of a time when she was badly bullied while at boarding school. Being a powerful physical medium and being just on the point of adolescence, she discovered how to create an elemental in the form of a wolf. She sent this animal out to frighten those who had hurt her, but after a while it turned on her and frightened her as well. She then had to dismantle the elemental, but before she could achieve this, she had to forgive all those who had hurt her. The Southern African Tokolosh is just such an elemental, and this too can turn on its creator.

Accidental elementals can manifest as poltergeists or other unpleasant ghostly creatures. I recently read of a man who took a job as an usher in a cinema and who began to see things when the cinema was empty. The first thing he saw was a man who walked across the space in front of the screen and then through the wall. His sensitivity allowed the spiritual entity to gain power, so before long, the "thing" attacked him, punched him and threw him around.

He told the cinema's manager about his experiences and the manager (who was aware that the place was haunted) called in a team consisting of a medium and an exorcist. They asked the usher to come too, so that the spirit would be attracted by his presence. What followed was worthy of a film scenario. The spirit of a dead person told the medium that when he was alive he had gone away to fight in the Second World War. When he came back, he discovered that the manager of the cinema at that time has taken his girlfriend. The young man had then gone home and fetched a souvenir Luger pistol that he had brought back with him; he went to the cinema and shot the manager.

The current cinema manager remembered that there had been a murder in the place almost fifty years before, and when the psychics and the usher looked it up in the newspaper library they discovered that the story was just as the spirit had told them. Apparently, the cinema manager at that time was a handsome scoundrel who liked to take advantage of naive girls whose men were away fighting in the war.

However, the spirits of the dead cinema manager and the Second World War airman who had killed him were not the real problem, because the thing that had attacked the usher was an elemental. This entity that had punched the usher, pinned him to the ground and even managed to inhabit his body while the medium and exorcist were at work, was something that had been created by the malevolent energies of the long dead seducer and his vengeful killer. Fortunately, the exorcist and medium cleared the spirits of the dead manager, the dead airman and the elemental, so that now the cinema is free of these sad and malevolent energies. Needless to say, the usher found work elsewhere!

I have a friend who lives with her divorced daughter-in-law and two grandchildren. The atmosphere between the two women is so venomous that the house is like a war zone. I have not heard of any elementals or poltergeists being raised in their household, but I won't be surprised if I start to hear of one once the boys reach puberty, if the household situation is unchanged when that time comes.

All my homes attract spirits. This is not really surprising, because any psychic is bound to draw them close. None of these entities are malevolent or unpleasant, and I don't try to shift them as long as they are happy to be around. If things change, we will call in our exorcist to shift them for us with bell, book, candle, crosses, holy water and so on. What fun that would be!

# 20

# Telepathy

I think the idea of telepathy has excited the scientific fraternity more than any other branch of the weird and wonderful. Scientists, government departments and other power-houses are fascinated by the idea of being able to read other people's minds or to send messages in this way. I recently read one report of a psychic who was invited to attend an interview by the CIA. When he arrived, he was taken into a room where - to his surprise he saw a large pig. The CIA man explained that the biological makeup of a pig is not far different to that of a human, and he then asked the psychic to use his mind-power to kill the pig by the force of his mind. The psychic promptly walked out!

Other scientific experiments are less dramatic than this, depending as they do on zener cards and similar things, but I am not sure that telepathy works in this way - at least for the majority of us. Most psychic happenings are driven by emotion, and there is little of that to be found when trawling through a mind filled with zener cards, a functionary who is reading a dry report in Saddam Hussein's private offices, or in the mind of a pig.

### *Telepathic tales*
Sally's daughter was on a fortnight's school vacation on a cruise ship in the Mediterranean, and as this was in the days before the advent of mobile phones, there was no way that Sally and her daughter could keep in touch. About ten days into the vacation,

Sally felt certain that her daughter was unwell. She didn't feel that the situation was serious, but she just knew that her daughter was not feeling good and she had visited a doctor. When her daughter arrived home, the first thing Sally said to her was "What on earth is the matter? Why did you have to go to the doctor?" Her daughter handed her a paper bag that contained the remains of a course of antibiotics, but Sally could see that her daughter had caught a bad cold and that she was suffering from a chest infection. Realizing that she was pretty sick, the girl had taken the sensible step of visiting the ship's doctor - and this had taken place at the very time that Sally knew it!

My daughter's first job was in a part of London that was half way between our home and an area where I worked in a part-time office job. On my workdays, I would drop Helen off in the morning and pick her up on my way home. I usually popped into the supermarket to pick up some shopping, so when Helen had finished her work she knew that she would find me there. On one occasion, I was right at the back of the large store with my head buried in the freezer cabinet, when, to my surprise, I heard a very loud "Muuum!" echoing inside my head. I made my way quickly to the entrance and saw Helen who was looking around for me by the store entrance. She had mentally called me and almost blasted my eardrums off from the inside!

Jenny was away in Australia when she was suddenly struck down with one of her very occasional asthma attacks. She was out in the bush with no inhaler and she didn't know what to do. Jenny fixed her mind on a spiritual healer called Graham and soon she started to feel better and to breathe more easily. A half-hour later, the asthma attack had cleared. Shortly after Jenny came back to London, Graham phoned her and asked her what on earth had happened. He had actually noted the time and date he had heard her call, and this corresponded exactly to Jenny's cry for help. Jenny gave Graham her heartfelt thanks for responding to her call so promptly and for sending her the healing that she had needed. They both laughed at the fact that they had managed to communicate over a distance of 12,000 miles and that Graham had been able to give Jenny the help she needed at that vast distance.

I remember once reading a science fiction book by the late John Wyndham, called "The Chrysalids", in which telepaths in New Zealand contacted children in Canada and saved their lives and ultimately the world. In the book, the voices were very faint and hard to tune in to - but the book was a fantasy. It appears that when a real telepath transmits over such a huge distance, it is no more difficult than making a phone call to someone two doors down the same street. No wonder governments are keen to harness this for themselves, if we consider the implications for contacting those in distant space ships?

### *Exercise in telepathy*

Make an arrangement with your friends whereby you will "call" them at a specific time. Ask them to sit quietly and tune in to your call. If they get anything at all, then you can take it in turns to send each other messages and even images, such as simple drawings and so on. This kind of thing happens spontaneously when friends and relatives think about each other, but you can try doing this deliberately. It may take several attempts before much happens, and it will also take time to discover who among your group are the best senders or the best receivers. Once you have this down pat, you can save a fortune on telephone calls!

A cheeky way of using telepathy is to focus on a perfect stranger who is sitting with his back to you. Sooner or later the person will turn round to see who is trying to catch his attention!

# 21

## A Psychic Selection

This chapter lumps together a number of topics, none of which are large enough for a chapter in their own right. Wherever it is appropriate to suggest things that you can try for yourself, I have included some instructions.

### *The sixth sense*

Extra-sensory perception or the sixth sense means anything that you can contact or experience that does not come through the normal five senses of taste, touch, smell, sight and hearing - or for that matter by knowledge or experience.

Those who work with in the emergency services or with the public in some other important way soon develop a sixth sense that is based on experience, intuition and sometimes more than this. A fireman may just know when a fire isn't an accident, even before he investigates it properly, a detective will feel when someone isn't being as honest and truthful as they appear to be, and a doctor might suspect that there is more going on than his patient admits to. As your own awareness develops, you will become more aware of people, places and things that feel right or wrong.

Follow your instincts, because they will not lead you up the garden path. For example, many people walk up the aisle looking the picture of happiness, but with their fingers mentally crossed behind their backs. Their intuitive feeling that this marriage will not work out well for them is usually well founded.

Animals and children are often intuitive, because they don't dismiss their feelings in the hopes that they are wrong. Intuition is akin to having a second pair of eyes - and they won't let you down.

### *Dreams*

Some people are aware that they dream, while others swear that they never do so. In fact, we all dream, and it appears that dreaming is necessary for our mental wellbeing. Interpreting dreams is a tricky business. There are plenty of dream dictionaries on the market, but they can disagree with each other, and while some take a psychological approach, others give traditional interpretations. Some dreams are so clear that their meanings are obvious to us, while others are not. Some are contrary dreams, in which the dream means the opposite of what it appears to be saying.

When you sleep, your normal self-censorship switch is turned off; also your guides find it easier to speak to you while you sleep. Some cultures believe that the soul leaves the body and goes on a journey during the night, and perhaps this is sometimes so. Whatever the mechanics of sleep are, dreams can be prophetic. When you become more used to being able to see a little way into the future, you will be aware of those times when a dream has a special meaning. Recurring dreams are important, so always listen to what they have to say.

### *Automatic writing*

I have never tried this myself, but I have seen it done and the writer produced pages and pages of scribbled garbage. Having said this, I hesitate to run any method down because we all work in different ways, and there may be people who really do get useful messages in this way. If you want to try this, perhaps in a development circle, take a large notepad and open your chakras. Ask for messages to be conveyed through you so that you can write them down. Turn your normal conscious mind off and see what happens.

## Beethoven and his friends

I once saw a woman on a television program who said that she wrote music that had been channeled to her by Beethoven and Mozart. She played a couple of pleasant piano pieces on the piano - but as with automatic writing, my personal jury is still out on this one. The same idea is said to work for art and artists as for musicians, so if you are a musician or a painter, try tuning in and seeing if anything comes through for you. You may at least receive a bit of help with your own creations, even if you don't manage to channel someone else's.

## Psychic palmistry

Real or "scientific" palmistry involves reading everything that one can see on a hand. It is a skill that anyone can learn and it doesn't require any psychic ability at all, although intuition and psychic abilities are always useful to a palmist. However, there is one method of hand reading that is entirely psychic. I have heard that it is sometimes used in India and China and probably among gypsies as well.

Take the person you wish to examine to a window or to some other place where there is a good light. Look into the palm and allow your eyes to drift out of focus a little. Your eyes will be drawn to the small lines in the center of the hand. After a few moments, these may appear to form some kind of shape that might tell you something about the person. This is not very different from tea leaf reading, so you could even use a tea leaf reading book to help you make your interpretations, but your own intuition will always be your best guide. The fact that you are holding a person's hand also helps you to create a psychic link.

## Witchdoctor's bones

I have a regular monthly radio program in which I talk about and demonstrate something different each time I broadcast. There are so many different methods of divination in existence that over a period of eighteen months, I have yet to repeat any of them. The program presenter has had to cope with me using him as a guinea pig for some truly weird and wonderful methods of reading, but the strangest by far was the day that I brought some South African witchdoctor's bones into the studio.

African Sangomas use a combination of clairvoyance and a carefully collected set of "tools" which include small chicken bones or the bones of other small animals, along with semi-precious stones, seeds and other bits and pieces. Each tool has a meaning attached to it. For example, one of the bones will refer to the client himself, while others refer to his partner, children and other people or outside circumstances that may apply in any reading. Some stones refer to the client's own natural wisdom and intuition while others indicate help from his ancestors. Yet others refer to enemies or problems of one kind or another.

The Sangoma and his client sit on the floor of a hut and the Sangoma recites invocations that put him into a light trance. Then the Sangoma asks his client to pick up the bits and pieces in his hands and to blow on them, meanwhile asking his and the client's spiritual guides and ancestors for assistance in the reading. Depending upon the kind of question that the client wishes to concentrate on, the Sangoma draws a particular shape on the ground. The bones are then lightly thrown on the ground. The way that they fall into the shape that the Sangoma has drawn on the ground and also in relation to each other takes him to the answer. Naturally, he also opens up psychically as well, so like all private consultations with a decent clairvoyant, this works very well. There is also a measure of healing in this kind of consultation, as the client will be able to talk over his problems and get them off his chest. If the client is sick, the Sangoma may give him spiritual healing or he may sell him some traditional medicine (called muti). He may also recommend a particular course of action - which may or may not be acceptable to our modern western minds.

### Flower reading

A rather nice method of reading is to use a flower. Ask your questioner to bring you a flower that he has cut or picked himself. Start from the bottom upwards, and "read" the condition of each part of the flower to see what is going on in his life. Patches of thin stem denote periods of illness, badly formed or curled leaves can indicate problems with childbirth or with children. Buds are new projects and the condition of the bloom shows the state of his future.

A bit of imagination will be needed here, but if you can also tune in on a clairvoyant level, you can make this work.

### Reading anything

The most popular tool for divination these days is the Tarot, but anything that can carry a system of numbers, letters and shapes can be read. You can do this by teaching yourself a system or by combining a system with clairvoyance. Many books on divination have chapters on reading such things as dice, dominoes and playing cards.

I have "read" beer-mats, coins from a person's pocket and crumbled potato chips (potato crisps to British readers). There are people who read tealeaves, coffee grounds, crumbled dried leaves and cloud patterns (especially in Africa). Others can read flames in a fire, pieces of card made from a variety of shapes and colors, and just about anything else that has a pattern, shape or system of dots, numbers, letters or colors.

This is not a book on divination as such, but any form of divination helps one to develop psychically, and it is also useful to fall back on when one's psychic energy is low.

### High-tech fortune telling

Here is something that nobody has seems to have thought of, but which I often use in order to see what kind of day I am going to have, in the same way that Rune Readers pull out a few Runes.

If you use a computer, you probably have that game of solitaire hidden inside it. You can call up a game of solitaire and read the seven cards that appear on your screen before you start to play. If you know the Tarot or if you have a book on it, you can transpose the Minor Arcana of the Tarot into playing cards by swapping Cups for Hearts, Wands or Rods for Clubs, Coins or Pentacles for Diamonds and Swords for Spades. Alternatively, you can buy a book that shows you how to read playing cards.

Any system will work if you use it regularly, although it will always be easier to read for someone else than for yourself, as you are always too close to your own problems to be objective or to bring through the requisite clairvoyance.

## *Apports*

An apport isn't something that you can do, but it is something that can happen. We all know what it feels like to mislay something and for it to turn up again later. Sometimes the missing item turns up just where we thought it should be, but sometimes the item turns up elsewhere. We tell ourselves that we must have been mistaken, that we must have moved it or perhaps that our partner, children or the dog must have moved it. But while we are busy trying to convince ourselves of a logical answer, we know deep down that the thing was where we left it, and then it wasn't - if you see what I mean!

A friend of mine told me that, only last week, she had put something down on a table in one room and then it disappeared, only to turn up again lying on the floor in another room. When things disappear, whether they turn up again or not, it might be due to an apport. In this case, someone moved the item, but who? And why?

Nobody can fathom the purpose of this kind of spiritual activity, but it is most likely to occur when someone is developing spiritually or when he is under stress. When there is stress, it is all too easy for us to blame ourselves for having mislaid or moved the item, but it may not have happened that way at all.

### *Superstitions*

Some psychics are very superstitious and others are not. I had one very good psychic friend who happily lived in apartment number thirteen, but others would never do so. If you look at the origins of the various superstitions, you will often find that they frequently started out from a basis of logic. It makes sense not to open umbrellas and wave them about when indoors, and after several accidents (especially when children wag umbrellas around), this became "unlucky".

My mother believed that it was unlucky to mop up spilled liquid with paper rather than with a cloth. I could see no logic in this, until a friend of mine who once worked in the printing trade told me that, in days of old, paper was extremely expensive. At that time, even scraps of wrapping paper were carefully preserved and paper was never used for mopping up spills.

A lawyer (solicitor to British readers) once told me that he opened his business on a Tuesday rather than a Monday because his mother had told him that Monday was an unlucky day upon which to start a business. This superstition may have arisen from astrology, because Monday is the Moon's day, so this is better for domestic matters than for business. Tuesday is Mars' day, while Wednesday belongs to Mercury, Thursday to Jupiter, Friday to Venus, Saturday to Saturn and Sunday to the Sun.

I would have recommended a Thursday to the solicitor, as Jupiter is associated with legal matters.

The southern Chinese hate the number four, because it sounds similar to them to their word for death. However, they believe the number eight to be extremely lucky for business and finances. Numerologists in Britain don't much care for the number eight, because while it is said to be good for business matters, it is also associated with hard work, hardship and disappointment in personal life.

If you wish to hang on to your superstitions, please do so. Newly developing psychics tend to see omens in everything, and they can go overboard with this, boring their friends and families to death. I only believe in good omens.

## *Magic*

Magic, spell-craft and witchcraft are huge subjects, so if they interest you, look for the many books that are available. Magic can be gentle and it can be dangerous. As with all spiritual matters, it is worth remembering that bad things always come back to haunt the perpetrator. Candle magic really works, and if it is of any help to you, my friend Leanna Greenaway has written a very good book called "Spellcraft & Magic" that covers gentle candle magic and several other forms of spell casting.

# 22

## The Heavy Stuff

There has been a tremendous boom in recent years in films and television programs that involve magic and the paranormal, and most filmmakers try to make these subjects nerve-wracking and exciting. Reality often work falls far short of these entertaining programs, but there is still no shortage of strange things to see and experience. So, let us now look at the really intriguing side of all things psychic.

### *Shape shifting and transfiguration*

There is a belief in Native American culture that an "adept" can turn himself into an animal for some special purpose, and once his mission has been completed, he can then transform himself back again into your everyday medicine man. A psychic can achieve something of the kind, but this usually involves him transforming his face into that of another person. This sounds truly weird - but it really does happen.

Just as a trance medium can take on the voice of someone who is speaking through him, some psychics can change their appearance. While a medium is in a trance, the face of the person who is being channeled through him seems to take over the face of the medium. This looks rather as though someone has slid a negative photograph of one person over that of a normal, positive photo of another. Sometimes the original face is still visible, but sometimes it is not. Some people are said to have such a gift for transfiguration that they can do it at a drop of a hat, but it is definitely not a common gift.

### Horny Ron and the horned beast

I have only seen a real transfiguration once and it was very intriguing indeed. I was working at a psychic festival that had been so poorly advertised that it was practically a washout. I became bored, so I wandered away from my stand (booth), and I sat down to chat with Ron. It is worth pointing out that this story happened several years ago, when I was younger, slimmer and a more attractive piece of womanhood.

Ron was a handsome middle-aged man who had a dark and dangerous Latin look. He enhanced his slim face, dark eyes and very black hair with a mustache and goatee beard. Ron was into witchcraft and also into quite a bit of devilment - and, as he really liked the ladies, he would go to considerable lengths to interest them. On this occasion, Ron gave me a Tarot reading and then he asked me if I would like to join his coven and to become his "acolyte". I knew that this would mean something that included unsavory sex and other things that I was not the least bit interested in doing with Ron - or with anyone else for that matter.

Ron spoke to me in a very low but rather commanding voice - all the while looking deeply into my eyes. After a few moments, I noticed that his appearance was changing. His face became more goat-like than ever and two small horns seemed to hover atop his head. His eyes changed from black to gold and the pupils changed from their usual round shape to slits. I don't know whether I was supposed to be afraid or turned on by this event, but I was absolutely fascinated. I sat quietly until he had finished talking, upon which the goat-face disappeared and Ron returned to his normal puckish self. For one moment, I turned over in my mind whether it would be worth joining Ron's coven to see this event again, but I quickly decided that once would have to be enough!

## *Exercise in transfiguration*

You can try to transfigure yourself. I can't guarantee a result as exciting as the Ron episode, but something might happen. If you are nervous, wait until you have a friend to chaperone you - and it might be handy to have a witness anyway. You can try this during daylight or you can wait until the evening, then draw the drapes and light a few candles.

- Find a mirror large enough for you to see the whole of your head and shoulders. Put this on a table so that you can sit comfortably in front of it.
- Now open your chakras. If you have a friend with you, ask him to open his as well.
- Sit quietly in front of the mirror for ten or fifteen minutes, while breathing deeply and evenly.
- Look at your forehead and try to keep your eyes open. Keep still.
- You should see some kind of change coming over your face. You may see your guide or some other shape begin to form. Your witness might be able to see this happening as well.
- Once you have finished, come back slowly to normal life and relax.

## *Another transfiguration exercise*

Do exactly as per the previous instructions, but face your friend. Focus on each other's foreheads and you may both see each other transfiguring. While doing either of these exercises, you may see one face appear or several of them show up in succession. These may be guides, you in past lives (or future ones), or anything else that feels like manifesting itself.

You may suffer from a headache for a few hours after doing this. I have read that if you place one hand on your third eye chakra and another on your heart chakra for a while, then reverse your hands, your head should clear. It's worth a try, but if it doesn't work, you can just take your favorite headache cure.

*Ectoplasm*

This word puts me in mind of all those sham and fraudulent mediums who operated in the 19th and early 20th century. These confidence tricksters hung up bits of gauze in darkened rooms and put lighted candles behind it, to make it look like something strange hanging around in the atmosphere. Modern people are too canny to be taken in by this kind of rubbish, because we see more convincing fake stuff every day on the television. Ectoplasm does exist, but it is not something that you can see very often.

Ectoplasm can look a little like mist combined with cigarette smoke, or perhaps a slightly sticky version of steam from a kettle. There are plenty of photographs that purport to show ectoplasm hanging around mediums, but I am not sure about these. More excitingly, some trance mediums can exude ectoplasm from their mouths or bodies during a séance, and I have witnessed this once.

A group of professional psychics happened to be working at a festival in England and, unsurprisingly, they decided to enliven a dull evening by holding a séance. They invited me to join them. The psychics arranged a number of chairs in a ring around the room, close enough to each other so that we could all hold hands, then someone placed one chair in the middle of the circle. Someone else put a dim red-colored light bulb that they had obviously brought along for the purpose, into a table lamp. This made the room fairly dark, but not so dark that we couldn't see each other.

A medium called Berenice opened the session by taking us though a meditation. Then a psychic called Zelma took the seat in the middle of the circle. For a while the room was perfectly silent. Then I became aware of a strange sound, which was something like wind blowing somewhere far in the distance. I noticed that Zelma's mouth was open and that a strange glowing white mist was working its way out of it. This mist wasn't like cigarette smoke, it was more like cold steam or light fog, and it hung in the air. After about five minutes, the cloud had extended about a foot in front of Zelma, and then it began to work its way back into her mouth again until it had gone. After this, the séance group moved on and others did their thing.

After the séance was over, I asked one of the mediums about this phenomenon. Apparently, the ectoplasm could have gone on to form itself into the shape of a person or perhaps into Zelma's spiritual guide, but on this occasion it only hung about and then went away again. The medium told me that it was dangerous to disturb the medium while they were producing ectoplasm, as this was actually created out of some part of their body. If Zelma had been disturbed, some of her internal organs would have become permanently damaged.

I have read that small pieces of ectoplasm can be left behind after such an event or that they can also hang around after someone has passed over, or it can be left behind after a ghost-busting session. It is said that it is cold and slimy to the touch. Those who touch it are likely to have some stunning psychic experiences, but they could also end up with some kind of debilitating ailment. I have never seen or touched anything like this myself.

### Seeing an aura or ectoplasm

If you try the transfiguration exercise, or indeed any deep meditation, you might find yourself picking up on an aura, or even seeing mist in the atmosphere. The fact is that all these weird and wonderful things are around us much of the time, but it takes practice before we can see them. Sometimes a major shock or upset in our lives opens the psychic gateway and starts us on the pathway to "seeing things".

### The very haunted hotel room

I thought I would end this section with an amusing but very true story. This involves my pal Berenice, who was the medium in charge of the ectoplasm experience. Berenice has a great sense of humor and she is good company, but she does seem to attract strange happenings. Oddly enough, Berenice and I were born in the same bed! This was because we both came into the world in a little cottage hospital (which no longer exists) to the north of London, in England. The hospital only had one labor ward, which contained one birthing table. We knew a third psychic who was also born in the same place, but he came to an untimely end and is sadly no longer with us. Whether that ward was known for producing psychics or not has always been a matter of great speculation to Berenice and myself.

Our story took place about fifteen years ago, on a cool Thursday night in late September, in the city of Bristol in southwest England. Berenice and I were both due to work at a psychic festival that was due to open the following day. We had driven down from the other side of the country in separate vehicles, and we had worked hard during the afternoon and evening setting up our stands for the forthcoming event. Tired and somewhat grubby from our exertions, we went out to a café for a meal with some of the other psychics, and then found our way back to the rather run-down hotel where we were based.

One of the other psychics was also staying at the guesthouse, and this was fortunate, because when we arrived, we discovered that neither Berenice nor I had our key with us. The other psychic let us into the building, but we had no means of getting into our room. We couldn't share with the other psychic because his room was a single and it was about the size of a broom cupboard. The office was firmly locked and there was absolutely nobody around who could have helped us. By now it was very late and we were very tired. We couldn't spend all night wandering the corridors of the place, as we knew that we had a heavy day ahead of us. We contemplated jumping into the car and driving to another hotel in the city, but we decided to look around first.

All three of us wandered up and down miles of corridors until at last, we came upon a door that was unlocked. Mercifully, this opened on to a room that contained a double bed that was made up. The windows to this room were wide open to the front car park and the room's closet was stuffed to bursting with clothes. It was all very odd, but by now, neither Berenice nor I cared much about the strangeness of the situation, as we were so exhausted. We closed the windows, took off our outer clothes and climbed thankfully into bed in our underwear.

Despite the fact that we had turned the lights off, the room seemed to be filled with strange light and energy. Berenice announced that it was definitely haunted, and proceeded to do a quick clearance on it. Even after this, there was still a strange blue light hovering over the other side of the large room and we both became aware of a strong smell of melons. To our astonishment, immediately below the suspended blue glow, we saw a man and woman dressed in 1920s clothing sitting at a dining room table and eating melons. This bedroom must have once been part of a dining room. By now we were too tired to bother with the melon eaters, so we just said goodnight to them and went to sleep.

The next morning, we got our room key, had a good wash, dressed ourselves and went out to work - this time with the key firmly tucked into Berenice's purse! We never did discover the secret of that strange room, because the office girl was new to the job and had no more ideas about it than we did.

# 23

## Psychic Self-defense

### *Raising the vibrations*

Opening chakras and performing rituals or visualization exercises raises your vibrations to the level that is required for the spirit world to be able to contact you. I can't stress strongly enough that you must close down after doing anything of a psychic nature, as this will lower your rate of spiritual vibration so that you don't continue to pick up vibes when you are not prepared for them. If you leave yourself open it will be hard for you to relax, sleep well and to live a normal life.

Just as you wouldn't go out in wet weather without being adequately dressed, you must "dress up" for your psychic activities, and "dress down" again for normal life once you have finished working.

Some extremely sensitive psychics don't like to face the direction of another psychic that happens to be working in the same room as them, because they feel that their central chakras are vulnerable to any vibes that might be floating about. This kind of thing doesn't bother me, but if you find it difficult to work alongside others, just turn yourself away from them. If you feel any kind of attack coming your way (even if this is in your own imagination), quickly close your heart chakra, because that is your most vulnerable area. A quick fix method for doing this is to imagine a pair of heavy green doors shutting tight, just about where your breastbone is located. The main thing is not to become paranoid about psychic attack.

### Primitive nastiness

I remember once reading with great fascination about Australian aborigine shamans who could "point the bone". Apparently, the shaman would use a specially prepared bone and he would point this in the direction of the person whom he wanted to destroy. The victim might be many miles away, but he would sicken and perhaps even die. When I first read about this, I thought was that it was no more than a fairy-story. Later, when I looked into psychology, I subsequently came to the conclusion that the person who thought he was being affected became so frightened that he talked himself into becoming ill. Nowadays, I know that a powerful shaman is perfectly capable of making someone ill without the victim being aware of the source of his problem. How these shamans cope with the karmic kickback from this is beyond me.

I have lived in southern Africa, where harmful witchcraft is common. The Africans believe fervently in the power of the tokolosh. A tokolosh can be a spirit person who looks like a dwarf or a child, who is sent into their village to plague them and to bring them bad luck. Other tokolosh magic involves putting some kind of doll or figurine into the victim's hut (especially under his bed) to cause mischief, so many African Sangomas make a good living out of clearing real or imagined tokolosh vendettas. I don't go into detail about any specific attack methods, as it would do more harm than good to print how they are done.

European witchcraft is full of stories of witches taking an enemy's hair from a hairbrush or collecting nail-clippings and impressing these into a wax doll that is then burned or otherwise destroyed. Modern witches only send out healing and blessings.

Nasty magic has no place in our world, but we can find ourselves on the receiving end of unpleasantness of a more ordinary kind, so it is wise to know what to do about it. It is extremely unlikely that a spiritual person would deliberately send out anything harmful, but perfectly ordinary people may bully us or get on our nerves. While it is not permissible to cause harm to anyone (even to an outright enemy), it is perfectly legitimate to protect oneself.

### Exercise in self-defense

When faced with an attack, imagine yourself totally encased in a suit of very shiny armor, or contain yourself within a golden egg, a silver tube or anything else that will protect your aura by reflecting bad vibes. Once you are safely encased in your imaginary protection, close your chakras - especially the central ones of the heart and spleen. Say nothing. Concentrating on this mental exercise means that you will tune out much of the nastiness anyway, because it is hard to focus on two things at once. After you have performed your mental exercise, don't retaliate, but simply walk away. The perpetrator will soon suffer some kind of setback some time later, from the vibes that return to him.

This kind of thing can only be a short-term cure, because eventually you will have to find some practical way of putting a stop to your tormenter's activities.

You may find yourself in a temporarily uncomfortable atmosphere where other people are arguing or stirring up trouble. Imagine a strong door between yourself and the other people, and close it tightly so that their aggravating behavior passes you by. Bear in mind that just as people can send healing vibes, they can also send harmful ones. Unfortunately, some people are more apt to dish out hurt than to be helpful. Be good to other people yourself, as long as you can do so without then taking undue advantage of your good nature. If you can't be good, then be neutral.

### Contamination

If someone has used your Tarot cards, crystal ball or any other tool without your permission, you may wish to clear the artifacts of unwanted vibes. The chances are that your tools will suffer no ill effects, but if you do feel the need to give your tools a quick "clean", mentally bring down white light from the universe and ask for your tools to be blessed and cleansed.

If you are still worried about a deck of cards, spread them all out all over a table, bring down lots of white light with blue (healing) flecks in it and allow this to flood all over and around them. After they have been cleansed, bless the cards and ask that they should guide all those who need help from now on. In a really severe case, throw Tarot cards out or even burn them and buy some new ones. I have only ever needed to do this once.

With solid objects such as a crystal ball or crystal stones, you can soak them in a natural source of running water for a while and leave them to dry outdoors in natural light. Then polish them and give them a blessing or meditate over them.

### Psychic clearance

If you simply cannot shift a bad influence by shutting it out, it may be that it has embedded itself inside you, so the techniques that I have outlined are not likely to be of any use. Find a psychic, a spiritualist or a witch who specializes in clearing psychic problems and ask them for help. If you don't have anyone to call upon, have a good few sessions of spiritual healing, Reiki healing, crystal healing and even such things as reflexology in order to clear your system. Even absent healing is better than nothing. Massage might help, as might acupuncture. Frankly, anything that works on the auric, etheric or subtle level will help.

### Tips for general forms of protection

When you travel away from home, soon after you have left your house, imagine a golden light coming down from the universe and filling every part of your home, the surrounding land, even burrowing deep under the foundations and covering the top. Then imagine this light developing a shiny crust that will shut out any harmful influences. This may be enough to keep thieves and other mischief-makers off your property.

If you are going through a bad patch and you need to improve your life, you can do this while you are inside the home, as the light will drive out any bad influences and make the home a safer and more pleasant place to occupy. Remember to fill the inside with light before forming the crust or you will keep the trouble in rather than pushing it out.

When you take a long trip in a vehicle, once you are inside the vehicle, call down the light and fill the vehicle with it. Surround the vehicle with light and then harden a crust around it that reflects bad vibes. Don't forget to protect every part of the vehicle or mode of transport, including its underneath area.

If someone you care about needs to take a journey that worries you, fill the person's aura with light and coat it with a reflective golden crust. If your psychic interests embarrass the person, you can do this for them, inconspicuously, without telling them. The usual rule with psychic work is never to do anything to someone else without his permission, but I feel that this kind of positive protection for your loved ones is permissible.

### *You haven't learned the lesson...*

One of the greatest dangers that can result from becoming involved in the psychic scene is the sheer stupidity that you are likely to encounter. By this I don't mean that someone will put a spell on you, but simply that his ideas are so silly and so poorly thought out that they are not worth taking on board. The following tale is one that upset me badly when it happened, although it is possible that it was meant to happen in the way that it did.

I was at an astrology seminar, giving talks and running workshops throughout the day. During a quiet period a woman approached me and said that she wanted to ask me about something that was happening on her astrology chart. I can't remember the details now, but I remember it showing a pretty horrendous planetary lineup that had been going on for at least a year and that was still in operation at the time of our conversation. While I was studying the chart, a plump young blonde with an air of supreme self-confidence bustled over and sat down, looking over the woman's shoulder at the chart. Then, in a voice full of self-assurance, she announced to the woman that "she must have needed to learn something important". She then went on to say that, as the poor woman had obviously not been prepared to listen, so the message was being rammed home twice more!

The woman's face drained and she was clearly mortified by this information. I was horrified. The woman had been through something dreadful and she didn't need this smug, self-appointed emissary from the gods telling her that she had earned, deserved or brought her problems down upon herself. The woman turned to me with a look of supplication. I told the young blonde to leave us and I then took on a counseling role. Perhaps the suffering woman's guides had sent the silly young know-all to us so that I would be encouraged to give some much-needed counseling. Who knows?

Where psychic matters are concerned, don't take stupid ideas on board. Be skeptical of everything that you read, see and hear. Prove things to yourself, filter them through your own common sense and personal experience and apply judgment before you accept anything. That goes even for the things that I have told you in this book - despite the fact that I have tried not to over-dramatize anything or tell you things that I don't consider true.

Counseling skills are very useful whenever one deals with people and their various problems. Although you are not obliged to be a counselor - there are always expert professionals available - you can easily come across a situation, like the example above, where it would be important to deal with the situation on the spot. I strongly recommend that if you intend to use your psychic skills professionally, that you also make the effort to learn at least basic counseling techniques. Otherwise, it is all too easy to give incorrect advice to someone who is open to suggestion, as is the case during a reading of any kind.

### *Location astrology*

This is outside the realms of psychic stuff, but astrologers know that certain geographic areas are not beneficial for a particular individual to live or work in. The theory is too complex to explain in this book, but the general idea is that the position of the planets on each person's horoscope creates lines that run around the earth.

If you happen to live in an area where a particularly unpleasant line happens to run, your life will not be easy. If you suspect that your troubles started when you moved to a particular area, it might be worth checking out your astro-cartography and local space astrology with an astrologer who specializes in this work. At the risk of sounding as though I am trying to sell you another book, if you are interested in this area of astrology, you can obtain details through my website (www.sashafenton.com) of my book called "Astrology…on the Move!" as this shows even a non-astrologer how to work this out. I mention this book, as there are few books on the subject, and so far, the others I have seen are very heavy reading unless you are an advanced astrologer.

A poor planetary line may be responsible for financial hardship or a disastrous love life that came about since you started to live or work in a particular area. Similarly, a history of dreadful vacations at a favorite family spot might also be down to your planetary situation in that place.

My second husband, Jan, and I first settled in West London. While there, I became ill and had a serious operation; we also struggled with finances, setting up our publishing business and we encountered many other problems. Once we left the area and moved to our current location, our health improved and our business took off. It may be coincidence, but the astrological lines are much better for us in Plymouth, where we are now.

### *Feng Shui*

The ancient Chinese art of Feng Shui has useful aspects, although some of it may be mythical. If you call in a proper Feng Shui specialist, he should make up a detailed Chinese horoscope chart for you and then help you to align yourself within your living space for the maximum benefit. Whether this realignment will fit the horoscopes of others who share your space is a moot point. Much of the Feng Shui that you see in books is pretty basic, but it won't do you any harm to use some of those ideas. Even if the Feng Shui magic itself doesn't really work, it will give you a feeling of having done something to improve your circumstances. Put it this way, even if it doesn't do much good, it can't hurt.

The only downside is that many Feng Shui experts charge a great deal for their services, so before plunging in, ask for references from those who have used the expert's services to ascertain the results. Better still, buy a few books on the subject and do what is necessary yourself.

### *Simple solutions*

If your home or workplace is making you miserable, wait until you have the place to yourself and take a white candle, put it in a candle stick and light it. Then take the candle with you while walking into every room, including the passages and bathroom facilities, and pray to your god or your guides for it to be cleared of any malevolence. If you understand American Indian smudging, do the same thing with the smudge herbs. Take care not to burn yourself or to start a fire. As always, you must take care of yourself and take responsibility for what you do, so a dollop of common sense will always be a welcome feature. For example, don't leave your front door unlocked, even if you have put protection on the house as outlined above!

# 24

## Checking out the Psychics

Part of your self-imposed training course should include checking out other psychics, including professionals, semi-professionals and amateurs. The benefit of training with a group or organization is that you can call on help from experienced members as you go along, but not everyone can, or even wants to, join a group or organization.

If you live in an area where psychics, palmists and any other "Readers" ply their trade, pay them a visit. Don't look upon having a reading as an indulgence, but consider the time and money as an investment. By being on the receiving end of such work, you will see for yourself the techniques that succeed and those that don't, and you will also begin to see how you might like to operate yourself.

### *Exercise for investigating*

If the people who you see have time to spare and if they are cooperative, ask them about their work so that you start to build up a body of knowledge and information. Don't expect a working psychic to drop everything in order to teach you, because they won't have the time for this, but snippets of useful advice will eventually add up to a useful dossier of information. You should actually keep a dossier, in the same way that witches note everything that they do down in their Book of Shadows. Try everything out and visit those who specialize in divinations that don't interest you as well as those that do, so that you can build up a wide body of knowledge. Don't take anything on board without thinking hard about what you have seen and heard, and always be skeptical of grandiose claims.

I have used the masculine terms of he and him throughout this book to make it easy to read, but the majority of people who are interested in psychic subjects are women. As one moves up the professional ladder, more men appear - and when one gets to the top of the tree, the practitioners seem to be divided just about fifty-fifty. Check out those who write astrology columns in your favorite magazine to see what I mean. The chances are that many of you who are reading this are female, so it stands to reason that you must take care when carrying out your investigations. On the whole, psychics, spiritual people, astrologers and so forth are a very gentle lot, whose main interest is to do what comes naturally to them, to help people and to earn a living. However, even in our trade there are rogues, and some join our business for nefarious reasons. The following suggestions are for your own safety, so please take them on board.

### *Safety first*
- Try to get recommendations from others before you visit any psychic.
- Never consult anyone who makes you feel uncomfortable, and don't go to any place that doesn't feel completely safe.
- If you are at all unsure or if you are visiting a male Reader, take a friend along.
- When you make the appointment, ask how much the practitioner charges, and what you can expect for your money.
- Ask if he will tape-record the reading for you or whether you can bring a recorder along and do this yourself.
- If the Reader objects to any of your reasonable requests, scratch him off your list.

- Spiritualist churches should be the safest places on earth, but even in this gentle arena there are sometimes lone men who are on the lookout for vulnerable females.

- Covens and witches' groups can be as gentle and harmless as spiritualist churches, but there are some that attract power-crazed people - especially male witches. Use your common sense, ask what you can expect to happen and consult someone who has been recommended to you by someone you trust, as being safe and worth the trouble.

- If someone suggests that you attend a séance, try to discover in general terms what you can expect to happen. The chances are that it will be far less exciting than you expect, but ask nonetheless.

- I do not apologize for repeating this: do take a friend along with you, certainly for a first appointment, as this minimizes any potential danger. Then, if either one of you feels uncomfortable and wants to duck out of the situation, one of you can develop a sudden crashing migraine and the other one can make the excuses. Genuine psychics will know that the headache is "political" rather than real, but genuine psychics won't give you any reason to feel nervous, so you are unlikely to want to leave.

### Beware of extras

A Reader, psychic or witch may offer to do something more in order to help you, and their offer may be completely honest and well worth taking up - or it may not. Sometimes a client will visit a Reader for a Tarot reading and then discover that he is also a crystal gazer or a Rune Reader. If the consultant is switched on, he might even hand the client a flyer that outlines his other services and his charges, leaving it up to the client to come back on another occasion if he wishes. This is a sensible approach and it works well for both parties.

- If a consultant offers to light a candle, say prayers, perform a ritual for you or send you absent healing, ask what he will charge for this. If he doesn't charge or if he charges a small fee for his time and trouble, this may be worth taking up. Use your own intuition to assess the Reader's sincerity and honesty. If a large fee is mentioned, decline the offer.

- Any consultant who offers to get your boyfriend back or pick the right lottery numbers for you, is either unrealistic about what can be done or he is a rogue. After all, anyone who can successfully pick out lottery tickets wouldn't need to work as a psychic in the first place.
- If a psychic frightens you by saying that someone in your family is likely to become sick unless you pay him a large fee for doing something about it, ignore this. The only thing that is likely to get sick is your bank balance.
- If you are a woman and a man offers you healing, massage or anything else that doesn't feel right, refuse the offer and leave the premises at once. Visiting a recognized healer is fine, but take a friend along on the first occasion.
- If a psychic starts to talk about sex in an inappropriate manner, get up and go home.
- If you feel unhappy or uncomfortable about anything at all, always leave immediately. There are plenty of genuine people out there, so you don't need to bother with creeps or advantage takers.
- The psychic doesn't need your address, but he may ask for a phone number if you call to make an appointment, as he may need to confirm this or to cancel if he can't make it. This should be perfectly all right, but if you feel uneasy, give him a cell-phone number and use a false name.

Don't pay over the odds for any service. Churches and psychic circles charge a small fee and this is understandable, as they need to cover their costs. Individual practitioners may work for anything from a small donation to a huge fee. I reckon that a reasonable fee is what you would expect to spend at a beauty parlor, or on a meal out for two people at a reasonably priced restaurant in your area.

I have come across one consultant who was an older retired lady who liked to be useful and to give occasional readings, and she passed a small fee on to the "guide dogs for the blind" organization. If a Reader is just starting out as a professional or perhaps trying to build a clientele in a new area, he may not feel able to charge a full fee just yet. These reasons are perfectly valid.

Some Readers advertise their wares at a very low price as a means of getting the public in. They give just enough to capture the client's interest and go on to suggest a higher fee for a more thorough job. The higher fee may be worth paying, but you must find out what their full charges are and what you can expect to get for your money. Readers are professionals, just as plumbers, electricians and dentists are, so you should always look into things before jumping in, but you should also expect to pay them properly for their time and their expertise.

### *Charlatans*

I have had many readings from many different kinds of consultant and I have long since come to the conclusion that some are better than others. The poor ones are not necessarily charlatans and they may mean well, but they are simply not very skilled or experienced. Too many psychics are amazingly satisfied with producing a standard of performance that is far too low. I haven't had any readings in America, but those who have (and those who work there) tell me that American Readers often give rather bland and generalized readings, due to their fear of being sued by malicious or advantage-taking clients. If this is the case, it is a shame, because the advantage-takers are obviously spoiling it for everyone else. Here are a few more points to watch out for:

- If a Reader tries to scare you, they may be trying to create the impression that they are better than they are. Some people "get off" on frightening clients and by dramatizing themselves. Don't go back there again.
- If a psychic starts the reading with rather generalized comments, give them time to warm up and get into the job.

If you show confidence in them, they will get over their initial uncertainty and warm up nicely. If the vagueness continues, it may be that they can't make a good link with you, but it may also be that they are useless. Give them the benefit of the doubt at first, and judge their performance after the reading is finished.

- If the psychic or medium asks you a string of questions, ask yourself what you are paying them for. On the other hand, there is no need to sit like "patience on a monument", saying nothing and testing the psychic to destruction. Confirm what they are saying with a nod or a few words. Mediums often need to pose a few questions at the start of a reading as a means of creating a link, but you shouldn't give much in the way of detailed answers back to them, as this can direct their reading.

You may expect or want one kind of reading, while the consultant may specialize in something else. A client may want guidance about his future, but find himself confronted with a medium who just passes on messages to the effect that granddad is happy on the "other side". Conversely, a client may want mediumship and find himself with an astrologer. Anyway,a good reading or sitting is usually worth having, even if it is not exactly what you expected.

### Too much of a good thing

Some Readers will give a reading and then get on to some bandwagon of their own. I have been on the receiving end of lectures about UFOs, religion or personal philosophy. I have also put up with those who ranted about the prevailing political situation. The worst offenders seem to be males who enjoy talking at a female audience. Again, you don't have to put up with this, so next time, try someone else.

### The client's responsibility

There is a level of responsibility that belongs to the client - although some clients wouldn't think this is the case. Some clients tell the Reader that they "don't want to hear anything bad". This means that they can only get to hear about part of their future, and they may miss out on a useful warning of an impending problem. Paradoxically, the client may phone the psychic back later and upbraid him for omitting to issue a warning. If a client asks for a reading, he should expect the Reader to tell him what is there and not to offer a sanitized version.

Sometimes a client will come back and say that something unpleasant that had been predicted came to pass, and the client may even have the temerity to suggest that it was the Reader's fault! The poor Reader doesn't create the client's future, he just tells him about it. None of us have the power to cause problems while giving a reading - or solutions for that matter. Putting solutions into effect correctly is the client's responsibility.

### Dial-a-psychic premium-rate phone-line readings

There have been stories about telephone organizations in Britain that were run by scoundrels who kept people hanging on the line and where the quality of the readings was poor. However, I think that word must have got around, or the premium rate regulating body proved to be effective, because these seem to have vanished from the scene. My niece worked for a phone-in organization for a while, and she received excellent top-up training to enhance her psychic powers and much testing of her Tarot skills before being let loose on the public.

I have phoned many different British organizations as a test, and they were all very good indeed. None of them tried to keep me hanging on the phone for an unreasonable amount of time, and the readings that the consultants gave me were as good as any I have had anywhere. I can't speak for the situation in your area, but it would be worth trying a couple of phone-in outfits to see what they are like.

One thing that I really do advise when using a telephone psychic is to ask him to look at a specific area of your life. Many people are unwilling to ask a specific question for fear of giving too much information. Other clients are afraid that by asking the Reader to focus on one area, he will miss out on something else that might be interesting for him to hear about. Leave the generalized readings for face-to-face encounters, when there is time for the psychic to go through every part of your life. When talking to a phone-line psychic, be specific about the area of your life that you wish to investigate. You may make a number of such calls during the course of your investigations, so you can vary the areas that you wish to examine with each call.

I can remember giving short readings at trade festivals where I worked for an organization that only allowed fifteen minutes per reading. I would ask the client what they wanted me to concentrate on, and many of them would say, "Oh, just see what comes up". Believe me, whatever a client says, there is always something specific on his mind. By the time I had latched on to what was really bothering the client and starting making some headway with the reading, the organizer would be ringing bells or tapping me on the shoulder to say that we had run out of time.

Don't expect any psychic worth his salt to give you a truly accurate timing for an event. A psychic or a Tarot card Reader can give accurate information, but often they cannot give an accurate time for a future event. If you really do need to know when something is going to happen, then rather consult an astrologer or a good numerologist.

Finally, if the psychic seems too confident in his assertions, or if he is too vague and unsure, he may not be any good. Either way, give him the benefit of the doubt once; see if his reading makes sense and if his predictions come true.

# 25

## Earning, Spending and Saving Money

### *Earning money*

Not everyone wants to become a professional consultant, but if you do wish to earn pin money or even become a full-time professional, make the effort to get properly acquainted with the ins and outs of the venture. There is always a lot to learn in a new trade, and pitfalls, both financial and professional. There may well be legislation in your area that must be observed, so do investigate thoroughly what you want to do.

For a start, there are many books available nowadays on starting a small business, which can give a lot of useful financial advice, especially in connection with the country or area where you live.

There are very few that are specifically written for the psychic and related types of work, so Jan and I wrote a book specifically to fill that gap. It is called Prophecy for Profit, and if it isn't available in your area, you can find it through any of the UK Internet bookshops, or else through my website (www.sashafenton.com) or our publishing website, (www.zampub.com). However, it is usually quicker and easier to obtain books from your local bookshop, and most of them will order any book for you. I am not trying to talk you into buying a book, but this book will give you the specific information you need to set up a divinatory practice. Even if you wish to give readings free of charge, you will find that book useful, because it explains how to avoid pitfalls that you would otherwise learn about the hard way.

### Spending and saving money

Meanwhile, here are a few considerations that I did not cover in that book. Those who are new to the psychic world often rush to buy all kinds of goodies. Years ago, it was difficult to find such equipment, but now there are plenty of new age shops and even mainstream outlets that sell such objects. Books are always worth buying, because they are relatively inexpensive and you can keep them for reference. Don't lend your precious books out to friends, because, in my experience, you probably won't get them back. If your friends are as keen as you are on these subjects, recommend a book to them, and let them spend their time, money and energy on this aspect of their development.

It used to be said that it is unlucky for a person to buy his or her own Tarot cards, crystal ball and so on. This is not true. You are the only one who knows what you need. The odd thing is that many people do acquire their first Tarot cards, dowsing rods or crystal balls as a gift, but after a while, they usually have to buy something else that suits them better.

Don't rush out and buy tons of expensive equipment. Think about what you really need. It is amazing how often we see people who are new to this scene buying up piles of crystals and semi-precious stones. They are pretty - but unless you can afford to buy them as mere ornaments, ensure that you do have some use for them. If you learn how to use crystals for healing, Feng Shui, magic or some other purpose, that's fine - but why be seduced into buying something just because someone wants to sell it to you?

You can make your own dowsing rods and pendulums, and the same goes for many other things. I have a wonderful set of Runes that I made from small stones that I picked up off our local beach, which I decorated with acrylic paint and some varnish. Such things as pentagrams, amulets and much else are easy to make, and they will be even more effective when you make them yourself, because you will have put your own energy into them.

If you see something that you just can't live without and if you can afford it, then treat yourself by all means, but don't necessarily expect it to work any better than a homemade object.

### Psychic festivals

In days gone by, psychic festivals drew in many thousands of people who were searching out information and equipment. Now, the Internet and the proliferation of goods on offer in all kinds of shops have made these festivals less attractive or necessary. The stands or booths at the larger festivals cost the earth to rent and this, along with the stand-holder's transport and accommodation, has to be recouped, so this is reflected in the price of the goods.

I recently read that quartz crystal bowls and Tibetan-type bowls are a great aid to psychic work and to healing. The idea is that you rub a cloth-covered stick around the inside of the bowl and listen to the sound that it makes. This may be true, but when you see these things on sale at festivals, your eyes will bug out at the prices. I wouldn't dream of suggesting that you avoid making any purchase, but please think carefully about what you really need before diving in.

### Is it value for money?

In Britain, charlatans and con artists are few and far between among psychic Readers, but I am not so comfortable about some of the goods or services that I see being sold in psychic fairs. Before you buy anything or sign up to a course, a treatment or anything else, look closely at it and refuse to swallow the blurb on the flyer or the salesman's patter wholesale. Always use discrimination before letting yourself in for anything. There is no need to consider everybody who works at such festivals to be a hobo or a thief, but take care.

If you have any form of healing in a psychic festival, ensure that there is enough space around the healing area for this to be effective. If thirty people are squashed together on narrow rows of chairs with healers working in a tight space behind them, this won't work well.

If a product claims to do something spectacular, ensure that it does what it purports to do before buying it. If you buy some unheard-of remedy, be sure that you are happy with its ingredients. Indeed, check that it has some ingredients in it, and is not just a bottle and pretty label (although it may be safer in some cases to buy something that does turn out to be water in a fancy bottle). Think of those traveling salesmen who roamed the Wild West selling snake oil before you lash out your hard earned money.

If someone wants you to sign up for an expensive course of training or some other on-going thing, ask for a list of people who have been on the course. Check that they aren't cronies of the organizers when you contact them, and then inquire as to whether the course delivered what it claims.

Don't become paranoid or mistrust everyone and everything, but do use your head. Draw upon your growing level of intuition, because if it can't save you from wasting your time of your money, what on earth is it for?

# 26

## And Finally...

I hope you have enjoyed reading this book, and that you keep it and refer to it whenever you need practical information on psychic subjects. If one day you meet me at some bookshop or psychic event and bring me your dog-eared copy to sign, that would be a pleasure; it is always good to find out that something I have produced has been useful to someone.

This book is unusual among others of its kind because I have tried to make it as practical as possible, which is not an easy thing to achieve with such a nebulous subject as psychism. I have purposely included some quite alarming information because I believe that ignorance is dangerous. I have pointed out where dangers lurk and shown you how to protect yourself from them. I haven't pulled my punches where it comes to buying goods or services from those who deal in them, either. I have tried to put your feet on the path of safety, security and of doing the right thing for the right reasons. I haven't gone in heavily on philosophy, morality or anything else of the kind, because I believe that we are all human, that none of us are saints and that we all make a mess of things or suffer the slings and arrows of outrageous fortune from time to time.

Other books on these subjects may be more spiritual, ethereal, mystical, inspirational, religious and saintly, but I hope that mine is practical, realistic and possibly a little hard-hitting in places. Before becoming a full time writer and then a publisher, I put in many years as a professional in various divinations, in many countries, so I know the reality of working in the field. Having said this, I am often astonished at the things that happen in connection with my psychic interests. I also know that a measure of balance, beauty and grace always comes along when we add the spiritual dimension to our normal lives. A really heartfelt prayer to our guides or gods can sometimes be a great help in times of trouble. We can ask for the strength to bear our burdens, and it can give us a feeling of doing something to help others or ourselves when nothing else can be done.

If you do take up psychic work, you will encounter people who are in emotional pain, so a course on counseling or psychotherapy might be advisable, as I have already made clear earlier in this book. Certainly, a measure of patience and common sense can do no harm. Watch your words, because people take them far more seriously than you think. If you don't understand that, remember some of the stupid or sarcastic comments that your schoolteachers made to you when you were young and vulnerable. They may have spoken without thinking, or may have come out with a sharp retort to make themselves sound clever, but you remember their words for the rest of your life. In exactly the same way, others will also take your words to heart, so take care.

Don't become obsessed with psychism and don't become a bore. Don't start to see omens everywhere, or suspect that you are under permanent psychic attack. Don't imagine that you are better than other people because you are "spiritual". If something amusing happens during a reading, then understand that spirit has a sense of humor. Don't start to take the spiritual world or yourself so seriously that you lose your sense of humor.

I wish you good luck as you travel along - and have some fun while on your spiritual journey!

# Index

Sangomas 112, 125
Scrying 77
scrying, Cloud 77
Séance 93, 134
self-defense 126
Sephirot 91
shamans 125
Shape shifting 117
Silbury Hill 41
sixth sense 109
Spiritualist churches 134
spirituality 13
St. Francis of Assisi 13
Stone Henge 41
Stuart 99
Superstitions 115

**T**
Tarot cards 44
Tarot, Rider Waite 45
Tarot, Universal 45
tokolosh 125
Totems 67
Trance 70
transfiguration 70, 117

**V**
vegetarianism 88

**W**
Watt, Berenice 17
Witchdoctor's bones 111
Wyndham, John 108

**Y**
yoga meditation 26

**Z**
Zelma 120
zener cards 106

LaVergne, TN USA
27 October 2009

162208LV00005B/108/P